sarah raven's
cutting garden journal

sarah raven's

cutting garden journal

F

FRANCES LINCOLN LIMITED

PUBLISHERS

Quarto is the authority on a wide range of topics.

Quarto educates, entertains and enriches the lives of our readers—enthusiasts and lovers of hands-on living.

www.quartoknows.com

Frances Lincoln Limited
74–77 White Lion Street
Islington
London N1 9PF
www.franceslincoln.com

Sarah Raven's Cutting Garden Journal
Copyright © Frances Lincoln 2014
Text copyright © Sarah Raven 1996, 2014
Photographs by Pia Tryde © Frances Lincoln Ltd with the exception of those listed on p192
Watercolour plans by Valerie Hill

Printed and bound in China
A catalogue record for this book is available from the British Library.

ISBN: 978-0-7112-3495-6

9 8 7 6 5 4 3 2

CONTENTS

FOREWORD

Here is a month-by-month journal format of my first ever book, *The Cutting Garden*, published nearly twenty years ago. This book was the foundation stone of all that I do now – growing, trialling and teaching people how to produce and arrange cut flowers in a direct and natural style. The idea of this new format is to help guide you on what needs doing, and when, throughout the year, and what is out there in the garden, looking at its best for you to harvest.

There are tips on picking (see pages 136 and 168) and conditioning (see page 74), as well as how to arrange your harvest (see page 70), but I always say, don't follow all that too slavishly. The best flower arrangements are often just single stems, with the colour and shape of the vase carefully married with the scale and colour of what you've picked. Then with thirty seconds of arranging you can have scent, colour and texture right by you on your desk, by your bed or in a series running down the kitchen table and you've then got the flower eye ball to eye ball. That's when you'll really get to know and love your garden and its plants, singling out one or two things at a time to revel in.

I'm happy to say I still love growing cut flowers as much now as I did then – the whole process from seed to vase, from selecting lovely things to grow to having them to arrange in your house and all in a matter of months if you choose the easy and quick-to-flower annuals and biennials. These are the plants I've concentrated on in the last twenty years – plants such as sweet peas (only the very highly scented varieties), my all-time favourite foliage plant *Euphorbia oblongata*, as well as plants such as marigolds, salvias, zinnias and the annual scabious. With these, the more you pick them, the more they flower. It's only when you go away – and forget to ask a friend to come in to pick your patch – that they will go over. They're the ever-filling cup, which never fails to deliver.

Sarah Raven, 2014

JANUARY

PLANNING A CUTTING GARDEN

Once you have been tempted to start growing your own flowers for cutting, you need to decide how much space you are going to devote to them, and this will depend above all on the size of your garden.

The cutting garden in spring

If you have a big garden with lots of underused space, the choice is wide open: you could opt for a small patch and cram it full of annuals; or you could go the whole hog and make a self-contained cutting garden. If, on the other hand, you are bursting at the seams and want to incorporate vegetables, children's swings and slides, a lawn and pretty herbaceous borders as well as flowers for cutting, the options are more limited: you could sacrifice one area to make a cutting patch; or you could integrate plants that are good for cutting into a mixed garden.

You will probably think next about your budget, but just as important is the question of time: the size of your cutting area must be geared to the amount of time that you are prepared to give. There is no point in pretending that stocking and maintaining a garden can be done in a trice. From the moment that the days lengthen in spring, you will be mulching, pruning, sowing, dividing, weeding and watering.

CUTTING GARDEN DESIGN

Before you put pen to paper in designing a cutting patch or garden, you will need to work out its exact size and where to place it. These, with some other considerations such as adjacent structures and planting, will determine the form the garden takes, and what plants you can grow there.

Choosing a site
Try to pick a prime site, in a sunny spot with good soil, because much will be demanded of this small area. Check that it does not have any fundamental problems, such as a frost pocket that will reduce your possible growing season, or a rain shadow from a nearby building that will increase the already considerable amount of watering that a cutting garden demands. You will need a convenient water source and, ideally, some form of irrigation system. Even something as basic as a leaky hosepipe, laid along the beds and plumbed into a water butt, is a useful device.

Surveying the ground and drawing a plan
Once you have decided on your site, you should draw up a reasonably accurate plan to scale. You need to do a detailed survey of the plot, seeing how it relates to other areas of the garden, and to nearby structures.

You should note on your drawing any noticeably dry or damp areas. Hedges and trees tend to suck up nutrients and water from a large surrounding area. Remember trees are the same size below ground as they are above it. Mark the shady areas, as well as those in full sun. Try to draw in the shadows thrown from surrounding buildings and shrubs and trees at different times of day.

In an ideal world you would allow enough time to observe the plot through each season, taking rainfall measurements at different points in the garden, and observing how frost and prevailing winds affect existing planting. Most of us are too impatient for that, but it should be your aim.

Finally, dig a good spade blade deep, to check your soil structure. Take a sample for pH testing. All these things will have a direct influence on what you plant and where.

The cutting garden in August

Once you have incorporated this preliminary information on your ground plan, you can draw up your design for the beds and permanent structural planting, such as new hedges and trees, and hard structures, such as paths and fences. Apart from matters of personal taste and finance, there are a few more points worth noting.

Beds and paths

Straight lines and clean geometric shapes are easier to work with than curving ones, and they divide more naturally into smaller sections. You will need paths to give you easy access to all the beds. The paths should be of generous proportions, too, as this is high-intensity gardening and you need to be able to get a wheelbarrow to each area. For the same reason, it is best to avoid steps in the cutting garden or plot. Paths of brick, gravel or stone might initially seem an extravagance, but will prove a worthwhile investment in the long run, as grass requires far more maintenance.

Walls, hedges and fences

It is well worth using part of your budget to provide some form of windbreak. Plants will grow better and quicker in a sheltered site. In the long term, consider building a wall, or the cheaper alternative of growing a hedge, to protect the whole area. As a temporary measure, hazel hurdles or closely spaced picket fencing are the most attractive alternatives.

For areas of particularly high-density annuals you might consider fencing around the beds so that you will not have to worry endlessly about staking and support, both of which are time-consuming.

JANUARY

SALIX *Willow*

Deciduous tree and shrub

ZONES: 5–9

HEIGHT AND SPREAD: *S. daphnoides* 7.5m/25ft x 7.5m/25ft;
S. caprea 10m/33ft x 7.5m/25ft; *S. x sepulcralis* var. *chrysocoma*
12m/40ft x 12m/40ft; *S. alba* varieties 15m/50ft x 7.5m/25ft

VARIETIES GOOD FOR CUTTING

Species such as *S. alba* var. *vitellina* (golden yellow) and *S.a.* var. *vitellina*
'Britzensis' (scarlet-orange) have brightly coloured stems. Pussy willow
(*S. caprea*) bears catkins from late winter. The female catkins are silky grey
and the male are grey with yellow anthers. Giant pussy willow (*S. acutifolia*)
has silvery catkins up to 8cm/3in long.

The smaller violet willow (*S. daphnoides*) is my favourite willow in winter for
its catkins, and *S.d.* 'Aglaia' is its best form. This is a loose-growing willow
with elegantly twisting branches and a fluid shape, which makes for relaxed
arrangements. It mixes beautifully with amaryllis and hazels.

CULTIVATION

Willows will grow anywhere with some
moisture (exceptions are *S. daphnoides* and
S. caprea, which do not need damp conditions).
When left alone, most willows will become large
trees, but you can coppice them and thus restrict
their growth. This will give brighter coloured
branches, but if done every year will reduce
the number of catkins, which are best on
wood that is at least two years old.
Compromise
by removing
half the stems
each year rather
than cutting them all
to the ground, and you will
always have vivid stems and
some flowers.

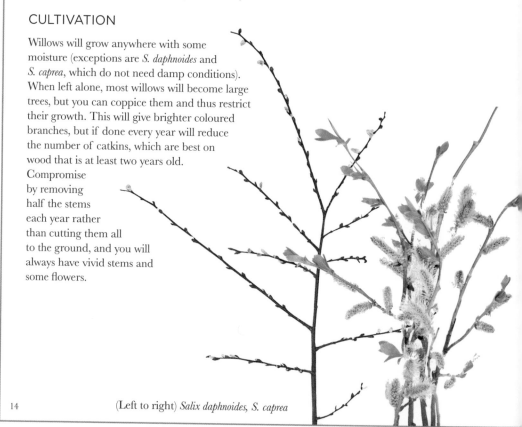

14   (Left to right) *Salix daphnoides, S. caprea*

HELLEBORUS
Hellebore, Corsican hellebore, Lenten rose, Stinking hellebore

Herbaceous perennial

ZONES: *H. argutifolius, H. foetidus* 6-9; *H. x hybridus* 4-8
HEIGHT: 45-60cm/18-24in x 30-60cm/12-24in

VARIETIES GOOD FOR CUTTING

All of them! Hellebores, with their fascinating forms and subtle green, pink and cloudy purple hues, are stars of the winter garden and winter arrangements.

Lenten rose (*H. x hybridus*) bears cup-like flowers in various tones of green, pink, claret, white and almost black. Some have beautiful freckling all over their faces. Choose plants in flower to be sure of planting colours you like and opt for those holding their heads horizontally (rather than modestly bowing), which are better for arranging.

Corsican hellebore (*H. argutifolius*) is the most vigorous. This serrated-leaved evergreen has open clear green flowers from mid-winter to mid-spring, and its seed pods make a sculptural addition to late winter and spring arrangements.

Stinking hellebore (*H. foetidus*) has lovely, hanging, green, bell-shaped flowers that look as if the petal edge has been dipped in a deep purple dye. Look out for the sweetly scented strain *H.f.* 'Miss Jekyll'.

CULTIVATION

All these hellebores are easy to grow. They like cool conditions with light shade and a heavy, rich, limey soil that does not dry out in summer. Plant them in autumn or early spring in well-manured soil and then leave them alone. Varieties will interbreed, so keep them well apart.

(Left to right) *Helleborus argutifolius,
H. foetidus, H. x hybridus*

PROJECT FOR JANUARY:

A WINTER FEAST

A relaxed, three-part table arrangement centred on large, festive candles uses foliage mixed with fresh, yellow and white winter flowers. The combination of the raised classical vase, complemented by glazed terracotta side bowls, and the bright bursts of informal flowers among waving spikes of old man's beard and violet willow, appears both simple and yet grand.

EQUIPMENT

- raised classical or formal vase, preferably on a plinth, about 38cm/15in tall
- 2 side bowls, preferably raised and matching the colour of the formal vase
- 3 ivory church candles, 40cm/16in long, for the raised vase
- 2 ivory candles, 30cm/12in long, for the side bowls
- 5 candle holders
- 3 florist's frogs
- 3 blocks of oasis
- florist's fix and florist's scissors

PLANTS FOR EACH SIDE BOWL

- 10 stems of hazel catkins (*Corylus avellana*), 30cm/12in long
- 5 arum leaves (*A. italicum* subsp. *italicum* 'Marmoratum'), each on a stem 15–20cm/6–8in long
- 5–10 cyclamen leaves (*C. hederifolium*), each on a stem 5–8cm/2–3in long
- 3 stems of *Clematis cirrhosa*, 50cm/20in long
- 5 stems of honeysuckle (*Lonicera* x *purpusii*), 30cm/12in long
- 5–10 stems of hellebore (*Helleborus* x *hybridus*, green and white forms), 20–25cm/8–10 in long

- 10–15 narcissi (*Narcissus* 'Cheerfulness'), 20–25cm/8–10in long
- 3–5 white fairy hyacinths (*Hyacinthus orientalis* 'Sneeuwwitje'), stems at full length

PLANTS FOR THE CENTRE VASE

5–10 stems, 60–90cm/2–3ft long, of each of the following:
- violet willow (*Salix daphnoides*)
- hazel catkins (*Corylus avellana*)
- old man's beard (*Clematis vitalba*)
- bird's foot ivy (*Hedera helix* 'Pedata')
- *Clematis cirrhosa*
- 15–20 cyclamen leaves (*C. hederifolium*), each on a stem 5–8cm/2–3in long

10–15 stems, 20–30cm/8–12in long, of each of the following:
- arum leaves (*A. italicum* subsp. *italicum* 'Marmoratum')
- hellebores (*Helleborus* x *hybridus* and *H. foetidus*)
- daphne (*D. laureola*)
- narcissi (*Narcissus* 'Cheerfulness')
- 15–20 snowdrops (*Galanthus nivalis* and *G.n.* 'Flore Pleno')
- 5–7 white fairy hyacinths (*Hyacinthus orientalis* 'Sneeuwwitje') or *H.o.* 'L'Innocence'

METHOD FOR THE CENTRE VASE

Use florist's fix to secure the frog in the bottom of the vase. Cut the remaining block of oasis to fill the vase as much as possible and so that it sits at least 2.5cm/1in above the rim. Place it on the frog and insert the 3 long candles in holders into the oasis.

Make the arrangement in a similar way to that shown in steps 1–3 for the side bowls. Start with the willow and hazel stems, making a relaxed but even arrangement around the candles. Insert the old man's beard, ivy, clematis, cyclamen and arum leaves, and then add the flowers, spacing them evenly to keep the arrangement open and light.

Once you have placed the finished vase and bowls on the table, scatter a few ivy leaves between them and, if you like, add some extra candlelight to the display by including a few small nightlight candles.

How to arrange each side bowl

1 *Use florist's fix to secure the frog in the bowl. Position the block of oasis on the frog. Place the candle in a holder and push firmly down into the oasis. Place the hazel stems around it, spacing them evenly in the oasis.*

2 *Insert the arum and cyclamen leaves. Let the clematis stems trail out to one side and balance them with the honeysuckle, leaving the stems long to keep the arrangement light, flowing and relaxed.*

3 *Infill with flowers, distributing them evenly but avoiding any rigid symmetry. The final effect should not be too dense. Remember to light the candles just before your guests are seated.*

EQUIPMENT FOR ARRANGEMENTS

1 **cone or funnel** for extending stems
2 **block of oasis** (23 × 11 × 8cm/9 × 4¼ × 3in) used by florists to hold stems in place
3 **water vial** to hold stem ends in medallions, wreaths and globes
4 **heavyweight pin-holders** in three sizes – 2.5cm/1in, 5cm/2in, 8cm/3in – to hold firm, average-sized stems in place
5 **glass marbles** to hold delicate stems in place, especially in glass vases
6 **glass stem-holder** to hold firm stems in place in arrangements in large shallow bowls
7 **florist's fix** use this strong waterproof glue-tack to attach florist's frogs, pin-holders, and so on, to bowls and vases
8 **candle-holder** (shown inverted) to insert into a block of oasis to hold a candle upright
9 **florist's frog or spike** to hold blocks of oasis in place

10 **gardener's twine** to make wreaths and tie bunches
11 **fine-gauge florist's wire** to tie in and bind stems in swags, wreaths, globes and medallions
12 **florist's scissors** to trim leaves, stem ends, etc.
13 **plastic sheeting** to protect the floor where you are working
14 **chicken wire** 30cm/12in wide to wrap around oasis in the construction of swags and globes
15 **watering can**
16 **globe of oasis** 20cm/8in to create globes
17 **moss** to line a hanging basket
18 **a pair of hanging baskets**
19 **heavy twine** to tie larger bunches and wreaths
20 **strong binding wire** to secure heavy swags and hanging globes
21 **strong hold-all** to carry all your equipment

JANUARY

TAKING HARDWOOD CUTTINGS

- You can propagate from many trees and shrubs by taking hardwood cuttings. Start with ivies and willows, which reward you every time by forming roots on every cutting you prepare. Then move on to the more difficult cornus and camellias, which are likely to have a smaller strike rate. Remove a woody branch, which in the case of willow can be as long as 1.2–1.5m/4–5ft, and insert it in soil lightened with sand in a prepared bed. For ivies, cut one trailing branch into sections with three or four leaves each. Insert these cuttings into a good sandy mix of compost and put them in a cold frame for the winter. If no roots have formed by spring, place them on a heated propagator bench to give them a boost – do this, too, for any trickier plants.

TAKING ROOT CUTTINGS

- Take root cuttings when plants are dormant in winter so that parent and offspring both have time to recover and flourish by the next growing season. This is the best way to propagate autumn-flowering anemones (*A.* × *hybrida* and *A. hupehensis*), pasque flower (*Pulsatilla vulgaris*), most of the eryngiums, acanthus and Oriental poppies. Mark the position of the parent plant in autumn, for the leaves will have disappeared by winter and, unless marked, you will have no idea where it is. Dig up the whole plant carefully, and, using a sharp knife, slice some of the root into 8cm/3in sections. Angle the end furthest from the crown at 45 degrees to tell you it is the bottom of the cutting.

- Have your pots of compost waiting, as the cut sections of root must not be left to dry out. Making sure you have placed each root facing down, tie a bundle together and put it into the compost. Cover with 2.5cm/1in of soil and place in a cold frame or a light, frost-free place. Replant the parent plant.

- By spring, shoots will have appeared on the cuttings. Check they have good roots and then plant them up individually in pots. Leave them where they are until autumn, when you can plant them out into the garden.

Camellia japonica 'Rosemary Williams'

JANUARY

FEBRUARY

STOCKING THE GARDEN

Once you have made all the structural decisions, it is time to start planning the planting design. One of the most fundamental questions you must ask yourself is whether you want shrubs, perennials and annuals all mixed together, or whether you would prefer to concentrate on one of these groups?

If your site and funds are limited, then consider stocking the whole patch with annuals. They require more work, but with minimal capital outlay. They will provide flowers in summer and autumn only, but you can always extend the picking season with spring bulbs. Remember, though, that if your plot is stocked mainly with annuals it is important to keep picking them, for they will stop flowering if the plants run to seed. So if you are someone who is away for a long spell every summer, then perennials and shrubs would be more suitable, as most continue to flower without deadheading or picking.

Crocosmia contrasts in a late summer garden

Another way to spread the cost of making a productive cutting garden is to invest the majority of your planting budget in shrubs during the first year or two, temporarily filling the area you have allocated to herbaceous plants with annuals. Then add perennial plants as you can afford them. It is always cheaper to grow them yourself from seed if you have the space to do so.

One of the great reasons for growing your own flowers is the range of possibilities it opens to you. If you see a flower that appeals to you, check its soil and sun requirements and, if they are suitable for your site, try it.

CHOOSING PLANTS

It is always worth keeping a note of the plants you particularly like and those you dislike whenever you see them in garden centres and other gardens. And if you are especially keen on particular groups of plants, such as those that are scented or those that will give you huge, statuesque arrangements, then note them as you find them. One of the chief joys of having a special cutting garden is that you can grow plants, such as flamboyant raspberry-ripple Parrot tulips, multicoloured cactus-headed zinnias and bright, zingy-coloured dahlias, that are fantastic in a vase but might be considered too gaudy for the general garden.

Plant lots of foliage plants as well as flowers. It is easy to forget the importance of beautiful foliage in completing an arrangement. As well as foliage plants, architectural plants should figure large in any list. They immediately make a group of flowers more dramatic. Acanthus, thistles, teasels, bulrushes, globe artichokes, and – in winter – dogwood stems and branches of catkins and pussy willow all add an extra dimension.

Before you make any final decisions about plants, you must make sure that the plants will survive in your garden. The type of soil, amount of sun and temperature extremes

will all have a bearing on your choice. It is no good expecting, for example, a silver-leaved, sun-loving, drought-tolerant artemisia to thrive in boggy shade. For the same reason, it is useful to list all your chosen plants in their site groups: those that do best in sun or in shade, in damp or dry conditions.

Armed with all this information, you can start to place the plants on the plan of your proposed cutting garden.

Balance of plants and colour

If you have decided to include a full range of colours in your garden, group the colours carefully to work well with each other. Concentrate the stronger colours in the foreground, with the whites and pale colours fading off into the distance. Don't try to have too many effects in one enclosed area. It is worth going on to draw out and roughly colour how this will look for every month of the year. You may find that at certain times there are some large gaps in the planting, or that there is a violent pink flower bang next to a scarlet one in the same month. Check your plan and concentrate on achieving a good balance between foliage and flowers at all times of year.

Go from the plan to the ground and back again, time and time again. If you fail to do this, it is all too easy to exaggerate or underestimate the actual scale of your garden and so be in danger of planting too much or too little.

Placing permanent planting

Except with the largest shrubs, always plant in groups. Aesthetically, this will give a more uniform and less dotted effect. Practically, if there are many flower heads, rather than just two or three, picking won't leave holes. Buy the larger herbaceous plants in threes, and the smaller ones in fives or sevens.

Aim to plant closer than you would in your normal garden. Particularly with shrubs, if you pick regularly and with attention to the shape and overall look of the plant, then you can use species that you may have considered too large for your garden, because the plants will always be well clipped. Even in a small patch you could think of including, for example, both a *Viburnum opulus* 'Roseum' and a smokebush (*Cotinus*). Look up heights and spreads as you plan what to plant, and simply space the plants slightly closer than their estimated span.

Having said all this, a common mistake made by people new to gardening is to underestimate the ultimate size a plant will grow to in a few years. Another mistake is to plant a tall, vigorous plant next to a much smaller, more delicate one, which will be swamped and die in a year or two. So always check sizes and also try to group together those of a similar vigour.

Note on nursery-bought plants

Don't be tempted to buy large pot-grown shrubs at enormous expense. You may believe that this will give you an instant garden, enabling you to start harvesting right away. In fact, mature plants tend to resent disturbance and may put on almost no new growth for a year or two. In this time a smaller and much cheaper plant may well have caught up in size. The same is true for herbaceous plants; a much more expensive 60cm/2ft plant is often less than a year older than a far smaller, cheaper one and may have just been potted on into a larger pot by the retailer for the new season. For a few months the larger plant will look more imposing, but again the younger one will soon catch up.

When you restrict the flower species in an arrangement, or the garden, you can run riot with colour.

FEBRUARY

FEBRUARY

CAMELLIA

Evergreen shrub and tree

ZONES: *C. japonica, C. × williamsii* 7–10
HEIGHT AND SPREAD: *C. × williamsii* 1.2m/4ft
× 2.5m/8ft; *C. japonica* 3m/10ft × 8m/26ft

VARIETIES GOOD FOR CUTTING

Some camellias drop their petals too quickly to be of use for cutting, but my favourites, the pure white single varieties such as *C. japonica* 'Alba Simplex' or *C.j.* 'Devonia' and, at the other end of the spectrum, the flamboyant raspberry-ripple, semi-double ones such as *C.j.* 'Tricolor', last well with buds still opening on a sprig a week after cutting.

I am less keen on the solid red and pink camellias – they remind me too much of plastic flowers in Mediterranean graveyards – but if you like these colours, go for *C. × williamsii* varieties. These, the easiest to grow, are the most reliable and hardy and drop their flowers as they brown and die; with some *C. japonica* varieties you have to remove the browning flowers by hand.

CONDITIONING

Just slit the stem ends before immersing in water.

CULTIVATION

Camellias grow well in lime-free (pH4–6.5), moist soil with good drainage and plenty of organic matter. Although they can cope with occasional windy blasts, they will suffer if they are constantly in a draught. They are ideally suited to sheltered, shady spots, such as walls that get little sun. Do not put them where they get early morning sun or the frozen flowers will thaw too quickly and go brown.

Plant during autumn or spring. Dig a large hole twice the diameter plus the depth of the pot and part fill the hole with peat (in the case of such acid-loving plants there is no alternative to using peat). Put in your root ball and backfill with soil mixed with leafmould or peat. This will give your plant a good start, and you will not lose your flowers.

In mid-spring, scatter blood, fish and bonemeal on the soil around the roots and then mulch with leafmould. For a good flower crop it is vital to keep plants well watered between midsummer and early autumn when the flower buds are produced. Otherwise they will drop without opening.

You can propagate camellias by semi-ripe or hardwood cuttings from midsummer to early winter (see page 20).

Camellia japonica
'Alba Simplex'

CROCUS

Corm

ZONES: *C. chrysanthus* varieties 4–9;
C. tommasinianus, *C. versicolor*
'Picturatus' 5–9;
C. vernus varieties 3–9
HEIGHT: *C. chrysanthus* varieties,
C. tommasinianus, *C. versicolor* 'Picturatus'
5–8cm/2–3in; *C. vernus*, larger-flowering varieties
9–10cm/3½–4in

Plant autumn-flowering crocus varieties in
summer, and winter- and spring-flowering
varieties in late summer or early autumn. Plant
them 5cm/2in deep and about 8cm/3in apart
in well-drained soil or short grass and in full sun.
I simply buy crocus bulbs and let them spread.
You can also propagate in early autumn by
seed or by dividing clumps of bulbs if these
have formed.

(Left to right) *Crocus
chrysanthus* 'Brass
Band', *C. versicolor*
'Picturatus'

CYCLAMEN

Corm

ZONES: *C. coum* 6–9; *C. hederifolium* 5;
C. repandum 7
HEIGHT: 10cm/4in

Cyclamen do well in rich, well-drained, friable soil
containing plenty of leafmould. Dry, shaded nooks and
crannies under trees or among rocks are ideal except for
C. coum, which prefers moist sun or part shade. Provide
protection against hard frosts in winter for *C. repandum*.
Topdress with manure and compost annually once the
leaves die down, after first raking last year's mulch
away. Take care not to bury the corms too deeply.
Cyclamen are great self-seeders, so just buy a few
corms and let them spread. Plant the corms in
late summer or early autumn, 5–8cm/2–3in
apart and 2.5cm/1in deep, flat side down and
tops still visible.

Cyclamen coum

ERANTHIS
Winter aconite

Tuberous perennial
ZONES: 4–7
HEIGHT: 5–10cm/2–4in

Like snowdrops, winter aconites are best divided and planted while still 'in the green', so beg a clump from a friend. Plant in heavy, reasonably fertile, moist but well-drained soil. They do best in alkaline conditions, under deciduous trees and shrubs where they can spread undisturbed.

Eranthis hyemalis

GALANTHUS
Snowdrop

Bulb
ZONES: 2–9
HEIGHT: 10–15cm/4–6in

Snowdrops do not do well if planted as dry bulbs, so if you are starting from scratch, persuade a friend to let you divide a clump. They increase rapidly once they are established, so you will soon be able to break up your own clumps. Always divide when the plants are 'in the green', that is just after flowering and before the leaves have started yellowing, usually in late winter or early spring. Dig deep under large clumps to lift them; split them by hand into smaller clumps and replant these at the same depth.

Galanthus nivalis

31

PROJECT FOR FEBRUARY:

FIRST SIGNS OF SPRING

This little vase of miniature flowers, one of my favourite types of arrangement, could not be easier to assemble. Each flower can be seen individually and, viewed close to, you can appreciate fully the different textures, colours, structures and scents.

Towards the end of winter the earliest bulbs, such as grape hyacinths, scillas, chionodoxas and miniature narcissi, begin to bloom in the more sheltered, sunny spots of the garden. Mix these with late-winter flowers such as pulmonarias, cyclamen, crocuses and polyanthus to create a brilliant, gem-like collection for your bedside table.

PLANTS

5–10 stems, cut as long as possible, of each of the following:
- crocuses, e.g. *C. chrysanthus* 'Brass Band' (yellow) and *C. vernus* 'Remembrance' (purple)
- pulmonarias (*P.* 'Sissinghurst White' and *P.* 'Blue Ensign')
- polyanthus (*Primula*) varieties
- scillas or chionodoxas
- narcissi (*Narcissus cyclamineus* or *N.* 'Canaliculatus')
- cyclamen (*C. coum*)
- grape hyacinths (*Muscari*)
- snowdrops (*Galanthus nivalis* varieties)

METHOD

Start with the more robust and fuller flowers, such as the crocuses, pulmonarias and polyanthus, to create your structure. Poke the finer ones, like the scillas, narcissi, cyclamen and grape hyacinths, in between these stems, making sure no single type of flower is too clumped together. Lastly, add the snowdrops.

JOBS FOR FEBRUARY

PRUNING

- Now is the time to prune, trim and tidy deciduous shrubs and climbing and large shrub roses, while the framework of the plant is most apparent. Most of the big shrubs will benefit from pruning in winter, as will any large rampant climbers.

- Start by removing dead, diseased or damaged wood right from the base, then concentrate on weak and spindly branches. Also, remove any suckers, as these will divert energy from the main plant.

- Always stand back and assess the overall shape. In general, aim for a balanced, even silhouette. Be careful not to destroy the graceful, arching habit of shrubs such as the species roses by removing no more than a third of their stems, although some vigorous shrubs, such as lilac, can safely be cut back harder.

SOWING SEED

- Sow seeds that are slow to germinate. The lovely, climbing *Cobaea scandens*, for example, should be sown from fresh seed in mid-winter if it is to put on adequate growth to flower that year.

- If you forgot to sow sweet Williams, lupins and hollyhocks (*Alcea*), do so now. You will not have such strong plants as those planted in late summer or autumn, but they will flower in the same year.

- If you did not sow your sweet peas during the autumn for storing in a cold frame over the winter, sow them now so they are ready for planting out in the spring. Pinch out their growing tips so you will have strong, bushy plants.

Prune roses
in February

FEBRUARY

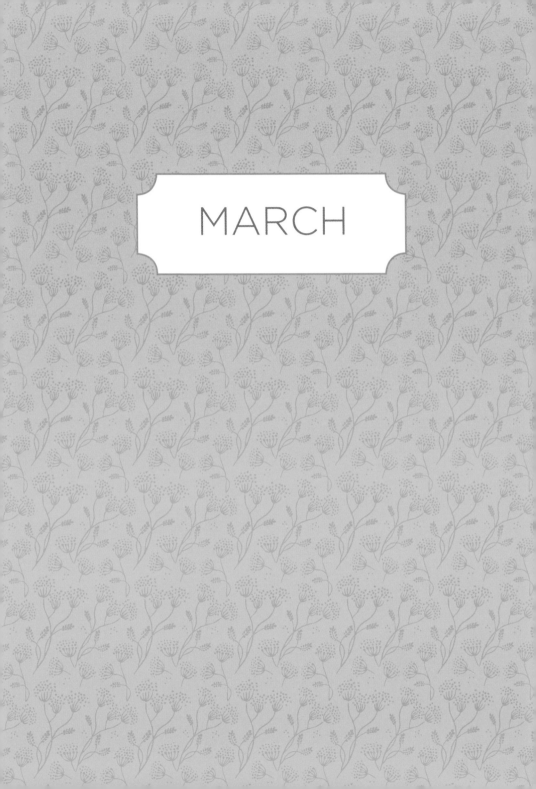

MARCH

CULTIVATING PLANTS

Stocking and maintaining a cutting garden that is both productive and beautiful involves a little work a lot of the time, with jobs best done for an hour here and there on a regular basis, rather than an occasional manic splurge for a weekend every few months. Try to gear the size of your garden to the amount of time you have to give it. There is nothing more depressing than beds and borders that were full of plants and promise in the spring looking like a wasteland or weed jungle by summer.

Growing your own plants from seed or cuttings or from rootstock division is time-consuming, but opens up huge possibilities barred to those who only garden out of a nursery or garden centre. If you grow your own, adding to what you already have from the vast and tantalizing choice of plants in the seed catalogues, it will cost a fraction of the price of nursery plants.

SPRING

This is the busiest time of year in the cutting garden. On a crisp, clear day you will be out there mulching, pruning and tidying. When it rains or it is freezing cold, you can take refuge in the potting shed or greenhouse and get on with sowing, pricking out and potting on.

As the season continues, picking in earnest will start. It is not compulsory to pick the spring flowers. Unlike the summer annuals, the spring bulbs and herbaceous perennials will be perfectly happy if you leave them where they are. You can either pick to your heart's content or leave your prize blooms to flourish in the garden.

General tips for sowing seed

- Sort your seeds into groups according to whether they are for sowing under cover or direct sowing into the ground, the month of sowing, the temperature needed for germination and any other special requirements.

Growing seeds under cover

1 *Gather all your equipment together on a bench at a good working height. You need seeds sorted in batches, seed compost, seed trays, single-cell insets, tall narrow legume pots, a soil compressor, labels and a soft pencil, a coarse sieve and a wooden spoon, and silver sand.*

- Always follow directions on the seed packet – for example, some seeds, such as lupins and sweet peas, have a hard protective coat and germinate more quickly if they are soaked overnight before sowing. And sow at the recommended time. Overtaken by beginner's enthusiasm the first year I started sowing seed, I began in the depths of winter, and my seeds under cover produced pale leggy plants that never did well, while in open ground many simply rotted before they could germinate. With a few exceptions, it is worth waiting for the days to lengthen so the seedlings have more light hours in which to grow.

- Mark all seeds as you sow them with a permanent label giving the name of the plant and the date it was sown.
- Use the finest spray or rose on your hose or watering can to water seeds in. Large drips or dribbles will dislodge soil and seeds, clumping them together or exposing them to the air.
- Don't always sow the whole packet. Just sow what you want for that year and store the rest for next. The germination rate may be slightly lower but will almost certainly be adequate. Fold the inner packet, label it clearly and store in a cool, dry place.

2 *Fill your trays with seed compost to 1cm/½in below the rim of the tray. Compress the compost gently with a block of wood the same width as the seed tray.*

3 *To moisten the compost, float your compost-filled seed trays in water until the bubbles stop. Leave the trays to drain; the compost should be moist but not dripping.*

- Remove slugs, snails and caterpillars using pellets, or by hand if you dislike using insecticide. They can munch through your whole crop in a matter of days.

Sowing seeds under cover

- Develop a routine for basal heating, watering, pricking out and potting on, making it as easy as possible, so that it is all done with regularity. For example, if you have a greenhouse, keep a hosepipe with the finest spray attachment sitting right by the bench.
- Good-quality plastic seed trays are easier to clean than wooden ones and will not twist and snap if you pick them up at one end when they are full of compost. Wash

them well at the end of the season and store them in the dark for next year. They soon become brittle if left out in the sun or light.

- For sowing and potting on, use the best-quality seed compost – a good mix of loam, peat, sand and slow-release fertilizer. You do not want a soggy peat bog forming, so check that the brand you are using is good and friable, or add some grit. Use a coarse metal sieve and a wooden spoon to get rid of any lumps. As a seedling tries to unfurl and grow, a lump may hold it back.
- Before sowing seed, gently compress the compost with a piece of wood to remove any large air pockets. Tiny

Growing seeds under cover (continued)

4 *Tiny seeds such as poppies are difficult to sow finely so mix them with silver sand in a ratio of about one part seed to six parts sand, to give you a better dispersed and more even distribution.*

5 *Sprinkle fine seed evenly over the seed tray. Large seeds such as eryngiums are best sown in rows, spaced so they can develop without competition. Sow plants with a long root run, such as sweet peas, in legume pots.*

rootlets are deprived of nutrients and water in air pockets.

- Whether you are using a windowsill, propagator or propagator bench in the greenhouse, you will fit more in a small area if you use square rather than round pots.
- You can use single-cell insets for sowing large seeds such as hollyhocks (*Alcea*), or for those that resent root disturbance, such as lupins, *Salvia patens* and cow parsley (*Anthriscus sylvestris*), as well as for pricking out and potting on. They allow for seedlings to be planted straight out. Peat pots are an alternative.
- Always sow into pre-moistened compost (see page 39). If you leave watering until

after sowing, you may wash seeds to the edges and corners of the trays, where they will clump together and grow less well.

- Never let your trays dry right out, or you will destroy the network of delicate rootlets.
- Covering the sown seeds with a polystyrene tile or glass wrapped in newspaper cuts down the light, and so helps many seeds to germinate (an exception is tobacco plant). It also reduces water loss as well as insulates and conserves any bottom heat from heated cables.
- Check every day for signs of germination. As soon as there is any sign of life, remove the polystyrene tile or piece of glass and move the seed tray to a position of maximum light.

6 *Cover seeds with a layer of sieved compost to the depth shown on the seed packet. Some seeds, such as tobacco plants, do not need covering. Label.*

7 *Place the trays or pots on a windowsill, in a propagator or on a propagator bench. Water with a fine mist spray and cover with a polystyrene tile, or with glass covered in newspaper, to cut down the light.*

41

MARCH

NARCISSUS
Daffodil, Narcissus

Bulb

ZONES: 3-9
HEIGHT: miniatures 15cm/6in;
full-size 30-45cm/12-18in

VARIETIES GOOD
FOR CUTTING

I used to have reservations about the huge yellow, or orange and yellow, trumpeted varieties of daffodils. I now love them, especially in grass, and they look fantastic all jumbled up together in a tall, white jug. I much prefer these unsophisticated flowers to the apparently overbred split-corona and double forms.

Of the miniature narcissi, the tiny Tazetta *N.* 'Canaliculatus' is lovely when mixed with other small-flowered bulbs such as scillas, grape hyacinths (*Muscari*) and polyanthus (*Primula*). Another good Tazetta is the lightly scented, pale cream *N.* 'Geranium'. Other narcissi I pick for their scent are *N.* 'Soleil d'Or' and the elegant and delicate pheasant's-eye narcissi, which have a particularly swoony scent in the evening. *N. papyraceus* is also especially fragrant, and it is easy to force indoors for winter.

CULTIVATION

Narcissi can be grown in any well-drained soil, in sun or even in quite shady borders. They are inexpensive bulbs if you buy them by the 50 or 100 from a good wholesaler. You will get bigger and better flowers if you plant them by the end of summer, as unlike tulips they benefit from being longer in the ground. Planted later they will do well enough, and even better the following year. They benefit from picking and deadheading, so the bulb does not deplete its food store trying to produce seed. After flowering, don't cut the leaves, or mow over them if in grass, until they have turned yellow. This allows the leaves time to feed the bulb to sustain it until the next season.

Plant the large forms 8–10cm/3–4in deep, and 10–15cm/4–6in apart; the miniature varieties should be 5–8cm/2–3in deep and the same apart. If you are planting in grass, use a tubular bulb planter or trowel to make a hole for each bulb. If you are planting them indoors for forcing, use a mix of two parts potting compost and one part sharp sand or horticultural grit.

Propagate by division, no sooner than six weeks after flowering; the clumps will benefit from being broken up every 3–5 years.

(Left to right) *Narcissus* 'Canaliculatus', *N.* 'Tête-à-Tête'

EUPHORBIA
Spurge, Milkweed

Evergreen and deciduous subshrub, annual, biennial and perennial

ZONES: *E. amygdaloides, E. oblongata, E. schillingii* 7-9; *E. amygdaloides* var. *robbiae, E. lathyris, E. marginata, E. seguieriana* 8-9; *E. characias* cultivars 7-10; *E. cornigera, E. sikkimensis* 6-9; *E. cyparissias, E. dulcis, E. polychroma, E. griffithii* cultivars 4-9; *E. palustris* 5-8

HEIGHT: *E. cyparissias, E. dulcis* 30cm/12in; *E. amygdaloides, E. polychroma, E. seguieriana* 45cm/18in; *E. amygdaloides* var. *robbiae, E. marginata, E. oblongata* 60cm/2ft; *E. cornigera, E. griffithii* cultivars, *E. palustris, E. schillingii* 90cm/3ft; *E. characias* cultivars, *E. lathyris, E. sikkimensis* 1.2m/4ft

This plant genus is certainly in my top ten – I use it with anything and everything. Its upright habit and vivid, acid-green flower bracts provide the perfect contrast in the flower bed and flower arrangement to all colours from pastels to richest ecclesiastical tones. For a succession lasting throughout the year, start with the shrubby evergreen *E. characias* varieties. *E.c.* subsp. *wulfenii* 'John Tomlinson' and *E.c.* subsp. *wulfenii* 'Lambrook Gold' are two of the best cultivars; both combine well with large bunches of fruit blossom. In early spring, too, there is the smaller *E. amygdaloides* and *E.a.* var. *robbiae*, which mix well with any bright tulips or a colourful bunch of *Anemone coronaria*. They are followed by the flat-topped *E. polychroma* and the taller *E. palustris*. One of the best mixtures is these two and the orange *E. griffithii* 'Fireglow' contrasted with black aquilegias and *Tulipa* 'Queen of Night'. In late spring I use *E. cyparissias* with its delicate, little, acid-green flowers and bracts in smaller bunches and posies.

(Left to right) *Euphorbia characias, E. amygdaloides, E. amygdaloides* var. *robbiae*

MARCH

ANEMONE

Perennial

ZONES: 4-9
HEIGHT: 20-23cm/8-9in

VARIETIES GOOD FOR CUTTING

Anemones are excellent for cutting in spring, summer or autumn, and even during winter. The wild wood anemone (*A. nemorosa*), with its simple Catherine-wheel flowers, is lovely on its own. Beautiful cultivars include the wisteria-blue form with buttercup-yellow anthers, *A.n.* 'Robinsoniana', and the double white *A.n.* 'Bracteata Pleniflora'.

A. blanda has a greater number of finer petals and flowers from late winter until mid-spring. Among many colour variants is the evening-sky-blue *A.b.* 'Atrocaerulea'. The *A. coronaria* cultivars are another spring mainstay for cutting. I like these best as single colours: the rich velvety, deep blue-purple, the zany carmine-pink and the pure white 'Die Braut' are all good, but they are

difficult to find unmixed. You may want to plant them in a trial area for one year, and transplant them into colour blocks in the next. I choose the single *A. coronaria* De Caen Group, not the double *A.c.* St Bridgid Group.

CULTIVATION

The *A. nemorosa* and *A. blanda* types thrive in dappled shade, in humus-rich, well-drained soil. They are particularly good for naturalizing in grass, spreading to form a carpet. If *A. coronaria* has full sun and well-drained soil, it will flower for months.

A. blanda, *A. nemorosa* and *A. coronaria* are cheap to buy as corms; these grow better if soaked for 24 hours before planting.

A. coronaria St Bridgid Group is grown commercially from seed, sown in spring, and flowering from late summer to the following spring, but the plants have to be kept above 8°C/45°F in winter.

(Left to right) *Anemone coronaria* De Caen Group, *A. blanda* 'Atrocaerulea', *A. blanda*, *A. coronaria* (De Caen Group) 'Die Braut', *A. nemorosa*

CHAENOMELES
Japonica, Flowering quince

Deciduous shrub

ZONES: 5-9
HEIGHT AND SPREAD: up to 3m/10ft, but plants are usually trained

Plant japonicas in well-drained soil in a sheltered, warm position. Prevent sparrows and starlings stripping the flowers of their fat blossom buds, to which they are very partial, by covering the entire plant with a fine mesh of black cotton. Cut back side shoots, or those growing away from the wall in wall-trained plants, to two or three buds immediately after flowering. This promotes strong, new growth to provide next year's flowering branches.

Chaenomeles × superba

HYACINTHUS
Hyacinth

Bulb

ZONES: 4-9
HEIGHT: 17–20cm/7-8in

Hyacinths like a sunny, open site. They thrive in any well-drained soil, preferably enriched with manure the previous autumn. For bumper flowers, give plants a liquid feed after the flower spikes have appeared. Hyacinths are cheap to buy in 20s or 50s from bulb wholesalers. Plant 8–10cm/3–4in deep, and about 20cm/8in apart, in autumn. I also force a lot of hyacinths to cheer up the house during the winter, both for cutting (fairy hyacinth) and pots (ordinary hyacinth).

Hyacinth orientalis 'L'Innocence'

47

PROJECT FOR MARCH:

A SPRING TAPESTRY

This array of mid-spring flowers and elegant glassware is inspired by the idea of pointillism, that dashes of colour create an overall image of richness and depth. Cut the plants to suit the heights of your vases.

Pick a selection of delicate flowers that look good close up. Add one or two vases of more robust flowers, such as the wallflowers and the hellebores, to enhance the delicacy of the rest.

Mix the violet stems with a few leaves in your hand and put them into the water all together. For the wood anemones,

EQUIPMENT

- glass bowls and plates, scent bottles, mini decanters and modern glasses
- 2 pliable twigs (e.g. hazel), 30cm/12in long
- 8–10 glass marbles
- 2.5–7cm/l–3in pin-holder, held in place by florist's fix

PLANTS

- 25 sweet violets (*Viola odorata*)
- 15 wood anemones (*A. nemorosa*)
- 9 flame-coloured wallflowers (*Erysimum* 'Fire King')
- 5 stems of *Euphorbia amygdaloides* var. *robbiae*
- 3 heads of *Daphne odora* 'Aureomarginata'
- 9 auriculas (*Primula auricula*)
- 1 plum snakeshead fritillary (*Fritillaria meleagris*)
- 3 heads of *Magnolia denudata*
- 7 young globe artichoke (*Cynara cardunculus* Scolymus Group) leaves
- 15 Lenten rose (*Helleborus* x *hybridus*) flowers and seed heads

first bend the pliable twigs into a zigzag, so that they form a web in the shallow bowl to hold the fine anemone stems upright. Use the strong stems of the wallflowers to provide a structure and then place the euphorbias in between.

Cut the daphne sprigs short and make sure their stem ends stay in the shallow water. For the auriculas, fill the glass to about a third with 8–10 marbles and poke in the flower stems, one by one. Simply place the fritillary and magnolias in their narrow-necked decanters. For the hellebore arrangement, use the pin-holder to place the artichoke leaves fairly evenly in the bowl, followed by the flowers.

JOBS FOR MARCH

BRINGING TUBERS INTO GROWTH AND TAKING BASAL CUTTINGS

- If you are buying tubers, never leave them in a plastic bag.

- Feel for any soft, diseased areas in the tuber, particularly around the stem, and look closely for mildew and scab. If limited areas are affected, cut them out.

- For early flowering, start tender tubers into growth under cover about six weeks before you expect the last ground frosts. Plant them out when the risk of frost has passed.

- If you want to take basal cuttings, place the tubers in a shallow tray and cover with a thin layer of moist compost.

- Remove the smaller shoots from the tuber. Cut away the lowest leaves and insert each new shoot in a pot of moist compost. Put in a propagator or cover with a plastic bag until roots have formed and the new tuber can be potted on.

PRUNING AND CARE OF CLEMATIS, SHRUBS AND ROSES

- Reshape plants that have become wild and unruly, congested in the middle, or insensitively or over-picked, by careful pruning.

- Cut out any dead, damaged or diseased wood.

- Cut back late-flowering clematis at the very beginning of spring. Prune to two buds.

- Hard-prune shrubs that tend to get woody and bare at the base.

- Cut back the side shoots of winter- and early spring-flowering shrubs, such as chaenomeles, to two or three buds, after flowering.

- When pruning Floribundas and other bush roses, start by removing any frost-damaged shoots. You may have to remove more at the end of spring if there are any late frosts. Remove suckers at the same time, slicing them off as near the original rootstock as possible.

- Always make cuts on rose branches at an angle.

- Make your cut just above an outward-facing bud. Choose a bud with two or three buds below it, so that if your chosen bud isn't healthy, there are others below that may be.

MARCH

APRIL

CULTIVATING PLANTS

PRICKING OUT

- At first, germinating seeds will grow an atypical pair of leaves. Once there are one or two pairs of true leaves (miniature versions of those on the mature plant), it is time to prick the seedlings out into a richer growing compost in a tray of individual cells. Hold on to the leaves, not the stems, at all times. If you bruise the stem, the seedling will die.
- Have a minimum and maximum thermometer on the wall to check your nighttime lows and daytime peaks. You must neither allow the temperature to fall below freezing nor let your plants bake in spring sunshine, although you do need the maximum amount of light. Ideally, avoid extremes in the greenhouse by having a thermostatically controlled heater and temperature-sensitive window vents, which will open and ventilate the greenhouse as soon as temperatures begin to rise. At the very least, keep a soil thermometer in the sand on your bench or do regular checks in your propagator or on your windowsill.
- Acclimatize seedlings gradually to the outdoors. If you are using cold frames, increase the length of time in the day that the frames are open, and leave them open on cloudy nights when no frost is predicted. If you do not have a cold frame, put the plants outside in a sheltered corner each day, bringing them in at night. Take care not to let the wind batter them and beware of the midday sun. Start leaving plants out all night when there is no risk of frost.

Pricking out seedlings and hardening them off

1 *Use a pencil or dibber to ease a clump of seedlings from the rest. Split the clump by hand into single plants, trying to keep a bit of soil attached to the rootlets. With your pencil, make a hole in the compost in the single cell and place the seedling's root ball in it.*

2 *Firm the compost around the seedlings and water them in to dislodge any air pockets. Label. Replace the seedlings on the propagator bench to recover for a week or two. After this disturbance their roots are at a delicate stage.*

3 *The seedlings are now ready to move to a cooler place where there is frost protection but minimal heat. If you have a cold frame, put them there. If not, place them in a sheltered corner of the garden each day and bring them in at night.*

APRIL

DIRECT SOWING OF SEEDS

- Many hardy annuals can be sown directly in the garden. Some, such as most poppies and lupins, resent root disturbance, so are best sown in their flowering position. Others, such as dill, bishop's flower, larkspur, marigolds, annual scabious, cornflowers, sunflowers and annual bupleurum, do just as well from direct sowing, which is of course far less time-consuming.
- If possible, start preparing the soil several weeks before sowing. Dig it over, weed and topdress or add organic fertilizer. Avoid mulching the area or you will then have to clear any mulch to one side to sow straight into the soil. When you are ready to sow, create a fine tilth by breaking up any clods of earth with a strong rake or a hoe.
- Sow seeds in short straight, zigzag or wavy lines. Seedlings in lines are easier to distinguish from weedlings.
- Always keep the area free of weeds, which compete with the seedlings for light, moisture and nutrients.
- Thin seedlings to just less than the distance recommended on the packet. Although the plants will bulk out and compete with their next-door neighbours, with the amount of picking you will do you can afford to plant them slightly closer together.

Sowing seeds outdoors (direct into the soil)

1 *Mark out lines (or areas) where you will sow your seed with sand of a colour that contrasts with your soil. Using a hand trowel, the back of a rake or a hoe, make a shallow seed drill to the depth recommended on the seed packet. Line the base of the shallow drill with sand to maximize drainage. Sow your seed into the base of the drill.*

2 *Replace the soil but do not firm it in, cover with more of the contrasting sand to remind you exactly where the seeds are for watering and weeding, and label with the name and date of sowing. Water the seeds in using your finest rose.*

APRIL

TULIPA

Perennial
ZONES: 4-9
HEIGHT: 20-23cm/8-9in

VARIETIES GOOD FOR CUTTING

Tulips make supreme cut flowers. So much so, that there is not a month in the year when they are unavailable in the commercial cut flower markets. In the garden, you can plan to have one tulip or another to cut at least throughout the whole of spring. I have no real favourites among the early Fosteriana or Greigii varieties, but the Single Early 'Prinses Irene', with its strong, vibrant orange base colour and violet-purple marking at the bottom of each petal, and the bicoloured red and yellow 'Mickey Mouse' can hardly be beaten. Another good one is the rich red 'Brilliant Star'. Coming after these are the Darwin Hybrids, the Single Lates, the Viridifloras and the Lily-flowered forms. An excellent Darwin Hybrid is 'Gudoshnik'

with its red-on-yellow marbling, and you must grow the dramatically beautiful, deep purple-black Single Late 'Queen of Night'. Of the Viridifloras, cream and green 'Spring Green' and green and orange 'Artist' are both unusual and stylish. The Lily-flowered varieties are also elegant, with curving stems and pointed silhouettes. I particularly like the vibrant orange 'Ballerina', which has the added bonus of a freesia-like scent. Try also 'Queen of Sheba' or 'Aladdin', both red with yellow margins.

Next come the Double Late forms. 'Uncle Tom' is a rich deep claret, but it is hard to beat the theatrical 'Carnaval de Nice' for style and panache.

In a class of its own, too, is the spidery *T. acuminata*. I often put a single stem alone in a tall glass. With the fantastic Parrot tulips we reach a climax. They look like a procession in a Guatemalan festival, their orange mixed with green ('Orange Favourite'), yellow veined with red ('Flaming Parrot'), white

dappled red and green ('Estella Rijnveld'), crimson and green tipped with scarlet ('Rococo') and deep purple-black upon black ('Black Parrot'). Nothing else in the garden can beat these in the glamour stakes.

CONDITIONING

Tulips last well in water. Strip the bottom leaves and tie the stems up in paper before soaking them for about eight hours. This is to keep their stems bolt upright: if floppy stems absorb water, they will stay bent, hiding their faces.

CULTIVATION

Tulip bulbs are cheap to buy from bulb wholesalers. Buy them by the 25, or, if you have room, 50 to 100. For easy picking, plant them in rows or blocks in your vegetable patch or cutting garden. Like most bulbs, tulips enjoy a good baking in the sun in summer and well-drained soil. Position them about

10cm/4in deep, and 10–15cm/4–6in apart, in mid-autumn. Left in the ground, they form bulb offsets that will eventually flower, but if, like me, you are too impatient to wait, buy more in each year. If you cut tulips very heavily, you may find that you exhaust all the bulbs, and few will flower the following year. So it is always worth putting in more tulips than you think you will want to cut, and then there will still be some flower heads to look at in the garden, and you will have more of a chance for a decent show the following year.

Once the leaves have died down by midsummer you can lift the bulbs to store until planting time. For ease I usually leave the bulbs in the ground, only lifting and dividing them every 3–5 years.

(Left to right) *Tulipa tarda*, 'Golden Melody', 'Hummingbird', 'Spring Green', 'Carnaval de Nice', 'Estella Rijnveld', 'Queen of Night', 'Artist', *T. acuminata*, 'Ballerina', 'Gudoshnik', 'Orange Favourite', 'Prinses Irene', 'Uncle Tom', 'Flaming Parrot', 'Texas Gold'.

FRITILLARIA
Fritillary

Bulb

ZONES: 4–9
HEIGHT: *F. meleagris* 25–30cm/10–12in;
F. persica, F. imperialis to 1.5m/5ft

VARIETIES GOOD FOR CUTTING

A primadonna among spring flowers, the statuesque crown imperial (*F. imperialis* 'Lutea') has tall, curving stems below a circle of huge, yellow, hanging bells. It is spectacular on its own or even better mixed with the 'Flaming Parrot' tulip and boughs of the horse chestnut's sticky buds. I also love the burnt-toffee-orange form *F.i.* 'Rubra Maxima' in a fiercely exotic mix with the other queen of fritillaries, *F. persica, Euphorbia characias* and shaggy 'Black Parrot' tulips. The only drawback to these fritillaries is their faint foxy smell, but I hardly notice it.

CULTIVATION

Fritillaries like deep, rich soil and prefer full sun, though *F. imperiali*s tolerates some shade. Grow *F. persica* in a well-drained site with the protection of a sunny wall. Avoid disturbing these plants and never cut them right to the ground. Topdress annually with well-decayed manure.

Snakeshead fritillaries (*F. meleagris*), cheap to buy from wholesalers, can be planted by the hundred in an area of unmown grass. Put in a conspicuous label (so you don't dig them up later on) at around 10cm/4in deep, and about 15cm/6in apart.

The larger, more expensive fritillaries do not flower until they are 4–6 years old so buy them from a good wholesaler, who will supply mature bulbs. Plant several bulbs 15cm/6in deep and 20–30cm/8–12in apart.

(Left to right)
Fritillaria meleagris var. *unicolor* subvar. *alba*, *F. imperialis* 'Lutea', *F. meleagris*

PRIMULA
Auricula, Cowslip,
Polyanthus, Primrose

Perennial

ZONES: 4-9; *P. auricula* 3-8
HEIGHT: 15-30cm/6-12in

VARIETIES GOOD FOR CUTTING

Primulas and polyanthus start to flower at the end of winter, beginning with the luscious Venetian colours of the Cowichan polyanthus. When arranged in separate, coloured glasses they look as rich as a church procession. The Gold-laced polyanthus, cowslips (*P. veris*) and primroses (*P. vulgaris*) follow. A primrose looks lovely in a shallow glass on its own, while the taller cowslip looks good in a wildflower display.

In mid-spring the auriculas come into flower. A creamy fluff (farina) covers the stem and buds. The petals often have a contrasting border as if wearing eye-liner.

To avoid birds getting to the flower buds construct a simple web of black cotton tied on short twigs pushed into the ground to stand about 8cm/3in above the flowers.

CULTIVATION

Gold-laced polyanthus, cowslips and primroses all need moist but well-drained, non-acid soil, in sun or partial shade. Auriculas require a grittier, alkaline soil and sun. All primulas and polyanthus can be grown from seed. If this is done early enough, you may have flowers the same year, otherwise buy at least five of any type to make a decent clump. Plant them 30cm/12in apart, and the gap between them will quickly close.

(Left to right) *Primula*
Gold-laced Group,
P. auricula 'Blairside
Yellow', *P. veris*

61

APRIL

SMYRNIUM
Alexanders

Biennial
ZONES: 7-9
HEIGHT AND SPREAD: 60-90cm/2-3ft

S. perfoliatum is an elegant plant with its lime-green bracts arranged like tutus up the stem, surrounding chandeliers of tiny, yellowish-green flowers. I like it best of all mixed with the fine *Dicentra formosa* 'Bacchanal' and the plum *Fritillaria meleagris*, on a brightly lit windowsill. The larger *S. olusatrum* is also good value when cut. With a chunkier, more robust feel, it combines well with the flamboyant Parrot tulips and crown imperials. Its one drawback is its quite unpleasant smell, so I use only a few stems at a time and would not put it in an enclosed room.

Strip the bottom leaves and then give it a good soak overnight. It will otherwise have a tendency to droop.

Smyrnium olusatrum

RANUNCULUS ASIATICUS
Ranunculus, Persian buttercup

Bulb
ZONES: 9-11
HEIGHT: 45-55cm/18-22in

These semi-tender bulbs come in glowing colours: from Burgundy red to marmalade-orange; to bright sunflower yellow with contrasting veining and edges. The double forms start like mini peonies, opening to look like big anemones. The singles are bigger and more glamorous. Use them in your spring multicoloured arrangements, mixed with tulips, anemones, ceanothus and euphorbias. Or simply arrange them in a tightly tied posy, with pussy willow and maple leaves.

Carefully strip all but the top leaves as they quickly go slimy on contact with water. The flowers will last up to two weeks in clean water.

Two cultivars of *Ranunculus asiaticus*

63

PROJECT FOR APRIL:

WOODLAND WITH PARROTS

These huge-headed, flamboyant Parrot tulips are best mixed with equally stylish and strong, or structural, foliage. Alexanders is perfect for this. To give height and lift to this robust arrangement, also use some maple branches, with newly emerged claret foliage and acid-yellow flowers to echo the colour in the tulips.

EQUIPMENT
waisted glass vase, 30cm/12in tall

PLANTS
- 9 branches of maple (*Acer platanoides* 'Crimson King'), 60–75cm/24–30in long
- 7 alexanders (*Smyrnium olusatrum*), 45–60cm/18–24in long
- 15 tulips (*Tulipa* 'Flaming Parrot'), at full height, about 45cm/18in long

METHOD
Arranging these ingredients could not be easier. The waisted vase holds the first few maple branches in place. The maples then provide both support and structure to secure the floppier stems and flowers of the alexanders and tulips.

So simply create a good overall structure and height with the maples, leaving the tallest branches standing about 1½ times the height of the vase. Do not make it too symmetrical, but it should look balanced at this stage. Next, poke in the alexanders, placing them fairly evenly throughout the arrangement. Finally, add the tulips, making sure there are no blank holes; with only one flower species used – and a powerful one at that – you need to give these tulips an even, but not linear, distribution.

JOBS FOR APRIL

SPRING PLANTING

- Start planting autumn-flowering bulbs and corms, new herbaceous perennials and tender shrubs.

- Plant gladioli, colchicums and nerines in mid-spring.

- Make successive plantings of gladioli corms every two weeks to get a longer summer and autumn flowering season.

- Snowdrops and aconites will establish and spread more quickly if planted after flowering, 'in the green'.

- Plant herbaceous perennials by mid-spring to give them time to form new roots before the rigours of flowering are upon them.

- Plant frost-vulnerable shrubs, such as rosemary and camellia, in late spring so that they are well established before next winter's hard frosts.

MULCHING, STAKING AND TIDYING

- Spread an organic mulch as soon as the soil begins to warm up. Do not mulch after a hard frost as you may trap any frost that is still in the ground. You can use forest bark, well-rotted farmyard manure, home-grown compost or redundant compost from a mushroom farm, spreading it to a depth of 5cm/2in. The garden will look immaculate at once!

- Avoid mulching plants that thrive in poor soil, such as dill and Algerian iris (*Iris unguicularis*), or they will produce lots of lovely, healthy-looking leaves and no flowers.

- Stake tall plants, such as delphiniums and eremurus, making a rough circle of canes or hazel branches around each clump, about half the ultimate height of the clump. As taller flower spikes grow, put in taller stakes to support these too. Tie garden twine or fisherman's nylon from cane to cane, making an almost invisible web of support.

- Heavy-headed plants, such as peonies, alstroemerias and phlox, are better supported with a mesh of hazel pea-sticks. Push these into the ground to leave a structure about half the plant's ultimate height. They will soon grow up through this web to hide it.

- Cut back any seed heads left for winter decoration, or dead growth left for frost protection, once you are sure that there are no more hard frosts coming.

TAKING BASAL CUTTINGS

- Cutting a young side shoot from a parent plant is a rewarding and easy way to build up stock. Now is the time to take basal cuttings from herbaceous perennials, such as campanulas, delphiniums and phlox. Use a clean, sharp blade to remove healthy shoots from the base of the plant. Thereafter, the routine is the same as for semi-ripe cuttings (see page 124).

APRIL

MAY

FLOWER ARRANGING

Don't feel intimidated – this school of flower arranging is accessible to everyone. There is no need for elaborate equipment or complicated techniques such as intricate wiring. All you need is a love of colour and a sense of drama. Bear in mind a few basic ideas on structure, scale and colour, follow the advice for cutting and conditioning, and you will be away.

Aim to create a heightened version of what is in the garden, with a similar feeling of natural ease and beauty: avoid strict symmetry and dominating vertical or horizontal lines. Remember that a flower arrangement doesn't have to be in a conventional vase. Create romantic globes with billowing flowers and branches of foliage; or construct enormous swags and medallions to hang inside or out. Keep the image of growing plants in mind, and have fun.

As well as creating average-sized bunches of flowers, think of making arrangements for both giants and pygmies. A huge vase of pussy willow, foxgloves or cow parsley is an impressive sight. At the other extreme, one velvety auricula, with a face like a mime artist, is almost guaranteed to lift the spirits. Don't rule anything out.

Blues, greens, whites and yellows make beautiful and peaceful combinations, but think, too, of mixing rich and powerful colours – oranges, purples and near-blacks, or crimsons, golds and royal blues. Balance their strength with calming acid-green or silver. Don't stop here either. Raise eyebrows by using colourful containers to make zinging combinations, such as fluorescent pink and turquoise or orange and lime-green. Above all, be brave and let rip.

When you restrict the flower species in an arrangement, you can run riot with colour. Don't be cautious: mix red, yellow, carmine, purple, blue and green to create a show-stopping display.

CUTTING

The best part of having a cutting garden is harvesting your own produce from your own garden. I fill my buckets with endless possibilities for colour combinations, gathering a bounty of all shapes and sizes. You can wander around surrounded by luscious scents, textures and colours all of your own making, and any of which can be brought into the house – the choice is yours. And, as you pick, all the anxiety and diligence that have gone into making your cutting garden will, I am sure, be metamorphosed into pride and pleasure.

If you obey a few rules based on common sense when you are picking, everything you cut from the garden will benefit and will have a longer vase life.

Cut when it is cool

You should always try to cut in the early morning or in the evening. These are the most beautiful times of the day, before the dew has fully evaporated, or when the last of the sun enriches the colours of the garden as a whole. During the day, particularly in the summer months with the increased heat, plants will transpire more. They will therefore probably be moisture-deficient and so more likely to droop as soon as they have been cut. Plants that have had the opportunity to restore their moisture balance overnight will be more able to withstand the trauma of cutting. To some extent the same applies when the plants have had some time to recover in the cool of the evening.

Invest in the right equipment

Good-quality secateurs and scissors will repay their price in years of service. They must be really sharp. If they are blunt you will crush the stem end and block it, and could damage the parent plant. If you are picking lots of flowers, invest in a trolley so you can push your buckets round the garden with you.

Don't hack away at your plants

Treat your garden with care. If you cut sensibly it is easy to pick enormous amounts from a garden without it being apparent that you have taken much, or even anything at all. Always try to pick from the back of shrubs and large perennials so that no obvious gaping holes are left near the path. Think of the overall shape of the plant as you pick from it and try to improve, not destroy, it. With smaller plants take one or two stems from several, rather than all the flowers from one and none from the rest.

Cut flowers in loose bud

Most flowers are best cut in loose bud. Ideally they should be showing some colour, but they should not yet be fully open. Find the stems on the plant with the most flowers at this stage. There will often be a flower or two that is more advanced, but this can be removed during conditioning if it has passed its best. The few exceptions to this rule include dahlias, zinnias and roses, where the flower will not develop fully from a tight bud. These must be picked when already fully out. At the other extreme some flowers – camellias for example – will come out from even the very tightest buds.

Cut your stems long

On the whole, the longer the stems, the easier the flowers will be to arrange. Cut each stem right down to the ground, or back to a main stem, so that you can make the most of

Equipment for cutting

- *Deep bucket, filled to one-third with water for long stems*
- *Shallow bucket, filled to one-third with water for short stems*
- *Empty bucket for the stripped leaves and side stems*
- *Trug or basket to carry flowers from the middle of a border to the buckets*
- *Thorn-proof gloves, for picking roses and blackberries*
- *Rubber gloves for picking euphorbias and rue*
- *Secateurs for cutting woody stems*
- *Folding knife for slitting stems and removing thorns*

the natural height of the plant. For a more three-dimensional arrangement, choose some twisting and turning stems as well as some of the more obvious, straight ones.

Leave bulbs with some of their foliage

Bulbs are the exception to the rule about cutting stems as long as possible, as they need some leaves left for photosynthesis to store energy in the bulb to carry it through the dormant season. If you cut lilies and crown imperials to the ground you will cut off almost all the leaves. So try to cut the stems leaving about a third of the main bulk of the foliage. Only once the leaves have browned can you cut them and tidy them up.

Don't leave cut flowers out of water
Once a plant has been picked, it should not be left out of water for a moment longer than necessary. This is most important in the heat of summer. Some plants, such as peonies, will never fully recover if they are left out of water, and their heads will droop. Others come to no apparent harm, but their cut life will be much curtailed. Keep one or more buckets one-third filled with water near you as you pick.

Keep your sizes separate
If you are picking both short and tall plants, keep them in separate buckets, or the taller, heavier plants will crush the flowers of the shorter, delicate ones. If their petals are broken or end up in the water, they won't be much use for arranging.

Strip the bottom leaves as you go
Strip the bottom leaves and side branches of each stem into an empty container as you go. If you remove them now, you will decrease the surface area that is transpiring and hence decrease the demands and stress on the newly cut flower. These leaves would need to be removed before conditioning anyway.

Think of arrangements as you go
As you pick in the garden, try to bunch plants loosely together, creating a balance of flowers and foliage, colours and textures. Particularly if you have a lot of arrangements to do, this could save enormous amounts of time, and it will avoid repetition.

Don't just pick the obvious
Use your imagination in what you pick. There will of course be flowers and foliage for picking that are self-evidently pretty to arrange. But look around for the less obvious, too. Check hedges, or any scrubby, wild parts of your garden that you hardly ever go into. Keep an eye out for interesting buds, seed cases, twisting or unusual coloured stems, berries and hips as well as flowers and foliage for your bunches. Just because some plant is not mentioned in this book, does not mean it will not do. Experiment with your picking. If a plant flops the first time, try searing the stem the next. Making your own discoveries will give you far more satisfaction.

Stripping and cutting stems
Strip the bottom third of your cut stems, taking off all leaves, side branches or thorns. Put the waste into a bucket and then on the compost heap. Divide your flowers into tall and short and keep them in separate buckets, so the larger and more robust ones do not crush the smaller, more delicate ones.

MAY

CONDITIONING AND AFTERCARE

Once you have gathered in your harvest, you need to put the flowers in a cool place out of direct sunlight, with a sink and a flat surface to condition them. After conditioning, leave everything overnight or through the day in deep water, so that the newly cut flowers have time for a good drink. Tepid water is absorbed better than water that is ice-cold, and it is a good idea to add some commercial cut-flower food containing nutrients and anti-bacterial agents.

Remove any leaves below the waterline
The waterline should always be kept just below the top of the vase and no leaves that will be below this should be left on any stem. Any leaf that touches the water will quickly decay and produce a bacterial soup, which will stink and clog up the stems and shorten the life of the other flowers. Too many leaves also put great demands on the flower stem of the cut plant.

All stems should be recut
Before you give your flowers their long drink you must recut the stems with really sharp secateurs, scissors or a knife. Cut them at an appropriate angle: for soft stems, cut at a slight angle so they don't sit flat at the bottom of the bucket; for woody stems cut at a 45-degree angle, thereby exposing more of the pithy centre for water uptake.

Sear sappy and soft stems
If you find that a plant you particularly like always seems to droop, even if you put it straight into water in the garden, try searing the stem ends in boiling water. This technique is particularly useful for sappy, soft-stemmed plants. Make sure that the flower heads are well away from the heat, either by angling the flowers away from the steam, or by wrapping the flowers in stiff brown paper. Dip the stems into 2.5cm/1in of boiling water for about twenty seconds. During this time you will often see bubbles emerging as the stem seals off. Then place the flowers immediately in tepid water.

Even flowers with tough but non-woody stems such as roses seem to benefit from this treatment. First cut their stems, preferably with a sharp knife, at a 45-degree angle. If the head has already flopped, which happens so often with bought roses, try searing the stems as soon as possible.

Hammer woody stems
The ends of woody stems of trees and shrubs should be crushed. Hammering the last 2.5–5cm/1–2in of each stem increases the surface area for water absorption and prevents a skin or seal forming over the stem end, blocking the plant's water uptake. Once the stems have been crushed they should be plunged immediately into a deep vase of tepid water.

Searing stems
The vase life of flowers with soft stems or stems that 'bleed' can be prolonged by searing them in boiling water.

Bind long, thin stems

Heavy-headed flowers with long, thin stems (such as tulips and dill) and greenhouse plants (such as gerberas) tend to bend after picking. If you leave them untreated as they suck up water in the conditioning process, the stems will become set in this bent position. Prevent this by binding the stems to hold them straight.

Support hollow stems

Hollow-stemmed plants with heavy heads may break under the weight of the flower head. To avoid this, gently insert a thin cane as far as you can up the stem. Fill the stem with water, then plug the end with cotton wool secured with a tight rubber band.

Ensure optimum temperature

Once you have gone to the trouble to pick, condition and arrange your flowers, it is worth doing all you can to prolong their vase life. Just as cut flowers need a cool place for conditioning, so they will last longer away from heat or direct sunlight. Research has shown that carnations held at 10°C/50°F age eight times faster than those at 1°C/34°F. So avoid placing arrangements near a radiator in the winter or in direct sunlight in the summer.

Add nutrients and preservatives to the water

What cut flowers need is a balance of sugars that can be utilized for metabolism, a substance to raise the acidity of the water and an anti-bacterial agent. Commercial sachets of cut-flower food contain agents for all three. It is worth going to a commercial market and buying them in quantity. Otherwise, add a few drops of bleach and a teaspoon of sugar to the vase and stir.

Make sure the flowers have clean water

Cut flowers last longer in clean water. Make sure you start with a pristine vase. Bacteria act on the cut ends of the stems, creating a slime which blocks the capillaries by which water is drawn up to the leaves and the flowers, so causing the plant to wilt. Check the water level every other day, as flowers will die quickly with only a tiny bit of water in the bottom of the vase. In hot weather you should try to change the water every other day. To do this, you do not have to destroy your arrangement: just leave the vase under a running tap for a couple of minutes and then replenish the cut-flower food. At the same time, you can remove any dead or dying flowers with your scissors to give the arrangement a face-lift.

Hammering woody stems
To prevent a seal forming and to increase the surface area for water absorption, crush the end of each stem.

Binding long, thin stems
If you want straight stems, they must be supported during the conditioning process.

PAEONIA
Peony

Deciduous subshrub and herbaceous perennial

ZONES: 3–9
HEIGHT: *P. lactiflora* and *P. officinalis* cultivars 60–75cm/2–2½ft

Peonies, like bearded iris, lilies and great swags of roses, always seem luxurious and extravagant to pick. My favourites are the deep crimson and carmine, double forms, such as *P. officinalis* 'Crimson Globe', *P. lactiflora* 'Inspecteur Lavergne' and, the darkest of all, *P.l.* 'Monsieur Martin Cahuzac'. I also like white *P.l.* 'Shirley Temple'. The single peonies, with their purer looks and great cup faces, look similar to waxen magnolias, and are also good cut. Sadly, the flowers of the shrubby tree peonies do not last more than a day or two, so I tend to leave them on the bush.

Peonies can be temperamental. Do not leave them out of water after picking, and pick them in bud or full flower.

(Left to right)
Paeonia lactiflora 'Sarah Bernhardt', *P.l.* 'Shirley Temple'

CLEMATIS

Evergreen and deciduous climber and herbaceous perennial

ZONES: *C. cirrhosa* 7–9; *C.* x *durandii, C. montana, C. tangutica* 6–9; *C.* 'Rouge Cardinal' 4–7; *C. vitalba, C. viticella* 5–9
HEIGHT: *C.* x *durandii* 1.8m/6ft; *C.* 'Rouge Cardinal', *C. cirrhosa, C. viticella* 2–3m/6–10ft; *C. tangutica* 3–3.5m/10–12ft; *C. montana* 6m/20ft; *C. vitalba* 9m/30ft

VARIETIES GOOD FOR CUTTING

There isn't really a clematis that is not good for picking, but the problem is their short flower stems. You can get round this if you're feeling brave and brutal by cutting one or more boughs of flowers. In spring, the *C. montana* cultivars are ideal for this treatment. They have strong, woody stems, covered from top to bottom with open, fresh-faced flowers, and are extremely vigorous and quick-growing, so they can take this treatment two or three years after planting. I use them often as the main feature in late spring and early summer bridal bunches. You can cut them long and trailing, and then bind them together to give you any length that you want. They will not last all day without water, but, if you make up the bunch just before it is needed, they will look fine for many hours. You can make a pretty and dramatic bouquet simply by mixing *C. montana* with *Viburnum opulus*, and using tall, curving Solomon's seal to form the crown. Clouds of white clematis bound one stem to another trail down the church behind the bride.

When making up a bridal bunch, a good tip is to do it in front of a full-length mirror, holding it as the bride will be, and putting in the flowers to be viewed from that angle. Leave the stem ends bare in water until just before the bunch is needed, then dry them as much as you can before wrapping them in clingfilm, followed by the ribbon or tape.

In summer there are lovely rich, velvety, red and purple clematis to choose from such as *C.* 'Royal Velours', while in autumn the yellows (*C. tangutica* and *C.* 'Bill MacKenzie'), and in winter the fluffy seed heads of old man's beard (*C. vitalba*) are mainstays.

CULTIVATION

Clematis are best planted in spring. Like most climbers, they thrive with their roots in shade and the stems climbing up a wall or tree, or over trellis in full sun. The montanas take shade and will grow to cover a shady wall. *C.* × *durandii* and others that do not cling are best grown in the herbaceous border or tied into a hazel or bamboo wigwam. All clematis like soil that is retentive of moisture, without getting waterlogged. For maximum flowers, feed regularly. Cut dead wood from winter, spring and early summer flowerers (*C. cirrhosa*, *C. montana*, *C. tangutica*) straight after flowering, shaping them at the same time. *C.* × *durandii* and the herbaceous clematis should be cut down close to the ground in autumn. Those that flower later, like the Viticella cultivars, should be cut down to within 30cm/12in of the ground, in late winter or early spring.

To propagate clematis, take softwood or semi-ripe cuttings from the cultivars, or layer them in early summer. For the species, sow seed in autumn. *C. viticella* self-seeds, although not rampantly.

(Left to right)
Clematis 'Elizabeth', *C. montana*

MAY

(Left to right)
Magnolia stellata,
M. denudata

MAGNOLIA

Evergreen and deciduous shrub and tree

ZONES: *M. denudata* 6–8; *M. grandiflora* 7–9;
M. stellata 5–9
HEIGHT AND SPREAD: *M. stellata* 3m/10ft
x 4m/12ft; *M. grandiflora* 6–18m/20–60ft x
12m/40ft; *M. denudata* 10m/30ft x 10m/30ft

Magnolia's luxurious, waxen flowers are all
spectacular for cutting. Pick a simple spray
of *M. stellata* to admire close to. *M. denudata* is
another beauty: pick just a sprig of this. Those
who have a spare expanse of south-facing wall
should consider the huge evergreen, summer-
flowering *M. grandiflora*. Or plant instead *M.g*
'Goliath', with its large, rich green leaves and
big, lemon flowers. The loose stamens of
M. grandiflora will fall out so you would do best
to remove these before arranging.

Magnolias thrive in rich, deep soil that is
retentive of moisture, but not boggy. They
need sun or semi-shade, and shelter from
strong winds. Mulch annually with rich
compost until established.

CONVALLARIA MAJALIS
Lily-of-the-valley

Deciduous perennial

ZONES: 4–9
HEIGHT: 20–23cm/8–9in

This is a plant that will grow where it wants,
so plant clumps of 10–15 crowns in early
autumn in semi-shade (although full sun and
deep shade will also do) and see where they
thrive. Planting lily-of-the-valley in different
sites in varying degrees of light and sun will
prolong your picking season.

If bought dry, lily-of-the-valley's long,
thong-like roots should be laid out about
2.5cm/1in deep, horizontally, and made as
firm as possible. They can also be grown
from seed sown in autumn.

Convallaria majalis

DICENTRA
Bleeding heart, Dutchman's breeches, Lady's locket

Perennial

ZONES: 3–8
HEIGHT: *D. formosa* 'Bacchanal' 45cm/18in;
D. spectabilis 60cm/24in

The fine, lime-green leaves, light structure and dangly, heart-shaped flowers of *D. spectabilis* 'Alba' combine beautifully with the Viridiflora *Tulipa* 'Spring Green', Solomon's seal and the lovely, white cherry blossom of *Prunus* 'Taihaku'.

Another favourite is *D. formosa* 'Bacchanal', which has delicate, velvet-crimson flowers over elegant, greyish, finely cut foliage.

(Left to right) *Dicentra spectabilis* 'Alba', *D. spectabilis*

SYRINGA
Lilac

Deciduous shrub and tree

ZONES: *S. microphylla* 5–8; *S. vulgaris* 4–8
HEIGHT AND SPREAD: *S. microphylla* 1.8m/6ft x 1.8m/6ft; *S. vulgaris* cultivars 5m/16ft x 2.5m/8ft

Many people refuse to have lilac in the house as it once meant bad luck. It would be a real pity to miss out on that delicious, wafting scent, so rid yourself of superstition and pick vast bunches of it. The most robust for cutting are the straightforward *S. vulgaris* varieties. I am not keen on the mauve forms, which look tinged with grey. I also tend to choose the single-flowered forms rather than the double, which can sometimes remind me of curly poodles. I like the pure whites, *S.v.* var. *alba* 'Maud Notcutt', which has larger individual flowers, and a smaller-flowered, dense variety, *S.v.* 'Mme Felix', which is famously good for picking and forcing. The small-flowered cream *S.v.* 'Primrose' is pretty mixed with early yellow roses. I grow too the reddish-purple *S.v.* 'Andenken an Ludwig Späth'.

(Top to bottom) *Syringa vulgaris* 'Andenken an Ludwig Späth', *S. vulgaris*

MAY

PROJECT FOR MAY:

A SPRING GLOBE

This is a combination of many of my favourite colours and plants. These fiery oranges, resonant black-purples, and pale and acid-greens recall the vivid colour schemes used in Titian's paintings. Imagine a line of these globes hanging above your head at a party overlooking the Grand Canal in Venice, and they should not feel too out of place. Hung en masse or singly, they will enhance any party, inside or, as here, in a romantic garden setting.

EQUIPMENT
- soaked oasis globe, about 20cm/8in diameter
- 90cm/36in length of 5cm/2in gauge chicken wire
- strong 3mm/^{1}/8 in binding wire
- fine-gauge florist's wire
- wire cutters and florist's scissors
- length of chain for hanging globe

PLANTS
20 stems, 30–35cm/12-14in long, of each of the following:
- alexanders (*Smyrnium perfoliatum*)
- *Aquilegia vulgaris*
- *Euphorbia cornigera*
- *Euphorbia griffithii* 'Fireglow'
- *Euphorbia polychroma*
- guelder roses (*Vibernum opulus* 'Roseum')
- 40 black tulips (*Tulipa* 'Queen of Night' and *T.* 'Black Parrot') 30–35cm/ 12-14in long
- 5 trails of *Clematis montana*, taking as much length as you can

1 *Assemble all the necessary pieces of equipment, tools, foliage and flowers. Cut a piece of chicken wire so that it will encircle your oasis globe, with a generous overlap. Cut a piece of the strong wire so that it is long enough to encircle fully the globe with the chicken wire wrapped around it, and add on an extra 30cm/12in length to make a loop to which you will attach the length of chain.*

2 *Bind the chicken wire carefully with the fine-gauge wire and string the piece of strong wire through the chicken wire right round the globe. Twist the wire ends several times; the weight of the globe will hang from this twist of wire so it must be secure.*

3 *Attach the chain with another couple of twists of the strong wire. Hang the globe at easy working height, so you can poke the flowers into the oasis without having to tire yourself by reaching up. Gradually cover the globe lightly with your first foliage plant,* Smyrnium perfoliatum, *spacing the stems evenly.*

4 *In the same way add the* Euphorbia cornigera *and* E. polychroma *and the guelder rose stems. Remember to check that the green oasis is well hidden at the bottom of the globe, too, as the view from underneath is most important.*

5 *Add the orange* Euphorbia griffithii *'Fireglow', the aquilegias and the black tulips, distributing them evenly.*

Add a few twists and turns of Clematis montana, *breaking any neat symmetry. Move the globe into position, hauling it up by attaching the chain to a piece of rope flung over a branch or beam or through a hook in the ceiling.*

STAKING

- Stake tall-growing annuals and biennials as well as any herbaceous plants that you did not stake in spring. Sunflowers, tithonia, onopordum, dill, moluccella and bishop's flower are among those that will need a hazel pea-stick or cane and string framework. The rule is simple: if it looks floppy or vulnerable, stake it.

SOWING BIENNIALS

- Biennials work best in generous drifts and, because they're grown from seed, this is easy to do without spending an arm and a leg. Try biennials such as sweet Williams, the massively fragrant *Matthiola incana* (perennial form), the delicate, black-leaved cow parsley (*Anthriscus sylvestris* 'Ravenswing'), the papery and elegant, Iceland poppy (*Papaver nudicaule* 'Meadow Pastels'), the ever-valuable foxgloves and the mauve columns of sweet rocket (*Hesperis matronalis*).

- Sow biennials, well spaced, into seed trays filled with any type of compost (see pages 38–41). You don't need seed compost – the seedlings won't be there for long. Sow each seed individually if you physically can; although this is impossible with tiny foxgloves and poppies, it is fine with the rest.

- Seeds should germinate within ten days and, if widely sown, there's no need to prick out the seedlings before putting them into the garden. You can separate them into individual seedlings from the seed tray, straight into their final planting site, or temporary resting position, and they'll shoot away.

- All but the Iceland poppy are happy to be dug up and moved around wherever you want later in the autumn or even next spring. The poppy needs more care and hates root disturbance, but the rest of these plants are tolerant, robust and easy to grow.

MAY

JUNE

MAKING A CUTTING GARDEN

If you decide to devote part of your garden solely to cut-flower production, you should ideally think about an area large enough to contain a mix of flowering trees, shrubs, climbers, perennials, annuals and bulbs. This will guarantee that there is something to pick all through the year. My own cutting garden measures 12m/40ft × 24m/80ft.

THE DESIGN

The rectangular plot is divided by brick paths into eight planting areas: four central beds and four L-shaped peripheral borders. It is contained by evergreen hedges on two sides, hazel hurdles on another, and, at the sunniest end, by an invaluable heat-retaining wall that supports a variety of wall shrubs and climbers. The central beds are generously proportioned; you should allow just enough space between plants to enable you to squeeze through them to pick from the middle. Evergreen planting includes four yews clipped into cones at the crossing, and lavender hedges lining the central paths. The trees also contribute a sense of permanence and vertical structure. Flowering cherries, an apple and a crabapple produce blossom and decorative fruit, an amelanchier brings spring blossom as well as good autumn leaf colour, and a sorbus provides bright, silvery foliage.

The large-cupped Narcissus *'Professor Einstein' is a good one for arranging on its own or cutting down to mix with blue grape hyacinths.*

THE PLANTING

The central beds are used for plants that change through the seasons. Bulbs are followed by annuals and biennials, which are simply planted between the lines of bulbs in hazy-edged blocks. A string line with permanent labels at each line end indicates where the invisible bulbs are when their leaves have died down, so that they are not constantly dug up.

The L-shaped beds contain more permanent plantings of shrubs, climbers and herbaceous perennials. These include winter-flowering shrubs underplanted with bulbs that flower in early spring, and a few evergreen plants to provide winter foliage.

MAINTENANCE

Maintenance is minimized by adding a thick mulch of compost or well-rotted manure as soon as temperatures begin to rise in spring when annual weeds start to germinate. Mulching helps keep down the need for watering, but regular watering and feeding are crucial, with high demands being made on plants and soil. The borders are hoed regularly to keep them weed-free.

These two Lily-flowered tulips – scarlet Tulipa *'Dynamo' (left) and yellow* T. *'West Point' (right) – have the pointed curving petals that give them the typical silhouette characteristic of this group of tulips. Each is tall, svelt and elegant, like the slimmest 1950s model. It is a shape that always adds flair and is very useful in breaking up a too-neat dome in any spring arrangement.*

THE CUTTING GARDEN IN SUMMER

In June the cutting garden is a mass of flower colour. Banks of herbaceous perennials provide a sumptous summer harvest, supplemented by the centre beds that are now brimming over with annuals. A wealth of foliage – shrubs, perennials and annuals – provides greenery to play a supporting role to the flowers.

STRUCTURAL FOLIAGE

Large shrubs planted for architectural and background foliage during the summer months include the silver-leaved *Elaeagnus angustifolia* and *Sorbus aria* 'Lutescens', the white-and-green-dappled leaves of *Comus alba* 'Elegantissima' with its striking red branches, and the spiky silver leaves of cardoon (*Cynara cardunculus*).

FOLIAGE FILLERS AND FLOWERS

The sunny bed in the near foreground has a grey-green pompon viburnum tree (*V. opulus* 'Roseum'), that provides glamorous and filling early summer foliage. Near it are spikes of acanthus (*A. spinosus*). Across the garden, the shadier L-shaped bed has a border of alchemilla (*A. mollis*), while stachys (*S. byzantina*) spreads on either side of the arbour seat.

All over the garden the euphorbias provide a brilliant succession of yellow and green and, in the case of *Euphorbia griffithii*, red, for mixing with greens, other orange-reds and blacks. Among the eryngiums are the steely silver Miss Willmott's ghost (*E. giganteum*) and the rich indigo-blue *E.* × *zabelii* 'Violetta'.

As the season progresses, the annual bells of Ireland (*Moluccella laevis*), dill (*Anethum graveolens*) and a late sowing of bupleurum (*B. griffithii*) supply armfuls of pretty and useful apple-green foliage well into autumn.

Shady perennial beds

Delphinium, Campanula pyramidalis, Rosa *'Souvenir du Docteur Jamain'*, R. *'Geranium'*

Centre annual beds

Black cornflower (Centaurea cyanus *'Black Ball'*), *snapdragons* (Antirrhinum) *and green tobacco plants* (Nicotiana *'Lime Green'*) *grow alongside larkspur* (Consolida *Exquisite Series*), *sunflowers* (Helianthus annuus), *amaranthus* (A. caudatus *'Viridis'*), *zinnias, tithonia* (T. rotundifolia) *and eustoma* (E. grandiflorum).

Centre

'Casa Blanca' lilies surrounded by pots of crinum lilies (Crinum × powellii), *rosemary* (Rosmarinus officinalis *'Sissinghurst Blue'*), *yew cones and artemisias* (A. arborescens *'Faith Raven'*).

Shrub and perennial L-shaped beds

Two large viburnums (V. tinus) *provide a backdrop to lavender, euphorbias and astrantia.*

Centre annual beds

Sweet peas (Lathyrus odoratus) *on tall wigwams go on flowering for many weeks. When the flowers are over, the wigwam is removed and then giant tobacco plants* (Nicotiana sylvestris), *mixed with a planting of the tall, daisy-like tithonia* (T. rotundifolia), *grow to fill the space and provide dramatic height for the autumn months. Other annuals here are deep blue salvias* (S. patens), *love-in-a-mist* (N. damascena) *and cornflowers* (Centaurea cyanus *'Blue Diadem'*), *while poppies* (Papaver rhoeas *and* P. nudicaule) *add splashes of red, pink and white.*

Sunny perennial beds

Bearded irises, Viburnum opulus *'Roseum' pompons,* Rosa *'Felicia' and* R. *'Iceberg',* peonies (Paeonia lactiflora), *cardoons* (Cynara cardunculus), *acanthus* (A. spinosus), *hollyhocks* (Alcea rosea *'Nigra'*), *euphorbias* (E. griffithii) fill these beds.

JUNE

PAPAVER
Poppy

Hardy annual, biennial and perennial

ZONES: 4-9
HEIGHT: *P. nudicaule* 35-50cm/14-20in;
P. commutatum 45cm/18in; *P. somniferum*
'Danebrog', *P. rhoeas* cultivars 45-60cm/
18-24in; *P. orientale* 'Ladybird' 60-90cm/2-3ft

VARIETIES GOOD FOR CUTTING

Many people think poppies far too frail
and fragile to survive cutting. Think again.
Poppies are some of the best flowers you can
grow in the cutting garden. The biennial
Iceland poppy (*P. nudicaule*) is the most robust
and long-lasting in water. Once the stems
have been seared, the petals will emerge
from tight buds and you will have a series
of new flowers for up to two weeks. The
best deep rich scarlet-orange forms are *P.n.*
'Matador' or *P.n.* 'Red Sail'. Use them also
in a flag-like, multicoloured summer swag.

Also perfect for several days' admiration
are all the wild corn poppy varieties.
Arrange the scarlet-red *P. rhoeas* on its own,
with its elegant, hanging, hairy buds and
stem, or mix it in a medley from one of the
mixtures (*P.r.* Shirley Group or *P.r.* Mother
of Pearl Group) of whites, pinks, mauves,
doubles and singles in an arrangement
of great delicacy and grace. Just keep the
vase out of the wind and away from open
windows. Grow some of the annual freaks
too, like the extraordinary *P. somniferum*
'Danebrog' (syn. *P.s.* 'Danish Flag'), with its
huge flowers with serrated petals in scarlet
and white. Also try the red with black-
spotted *P. commutatum* 'Ladybird', which
looks exactly as it should.

The perennial Oriental poppies
(*P. orientale*) will hold on to their petals for
several days if seared as soon as picked.

Plunge the cut ends into boiling water for
twenty seconds and then into tepid water
for a long drink. *P. nudicaule* buds may need
helping out of their tight calyces, which if
torn in one place will gradually unravel.

These are easy plants to grow in sun or
semi-shade, in moist but well-drained soil.
Plant the annuals and biennials in generous
clumps in the border, at 25–30cm/10–12in
spacings. Plant the perennials in groups of
three, 45cm/18in apart. The hardy annuals
can be sown either in autumn or in spring.

(Left to right) *Papaver nudicaule*
'Matador', *P. orientale*, *P. rhoeas*,
P. somniferum 'Danebrog'

ALLIUM
Ornamental onion

Bulbous perennial

ZONES: *A. aflatunense, A. cristophii, Nectaroscordum siculum* 4–10; *A. cernuum, A. sphaerocephalon* 3–8; *A. flavum* 3–9; *A. giganteum, A.* 'Globemaster', *A. narcissiflorum* 6–10; *Triteleia hyacinthina* 5–10
HEIGHT: *A. narcissiflorum* to 30cm/12in; *A. cernuum, A. cristophii, A. flavum* 30–70cm/12–28in; *A. sphaerocephalon* to 90cm/3ft; *A.* 'Globemaster' 0.9–1.2m/3–4ft; *Nectaroscordum siculum, Triteleia hyacinthina* 1.2m/4ft; *A. aflatunense* 1.5m/5ft; *A. giganteum* 2m/7ft

(Left to right) *Allium cernuum, A. cristophii, A. giganteum*

VARIETIES GOOD FOR CUTTING

There are so many excellent alliums for cutting that it is impossible to mention them all. Together they look like a starry globe of exploding fireworks. *A. cristophii*, with its green-centred, spiny stars, *A. giganteum* and *A.* 'Globemaster' are the largest and most impressive. Grow these for combining in a giant arrangement. Use the melon-sized globes of *A. giganteum* with heavy-headed, deliciously scented, white lilies such as *Lilium* 'Casa Blanca' to counteract the indisputably oniony smell of the allium as it ages. What is more, both flowers will continue to look good for 10–14 days, without any rearranging. Just change the water every other day. For similar, slightly smaller flowers, up to six weeks earlier, plant *A. aflatunense*.

Among the shorter-stemmed and smaller-headed varieties, grow *A. sphaerocephalon*. Its magenta-purple, shuttlecock-shaped heads are beautiful with whites and greens, or in a mixture of hotter colours. Look out, too, for the lemon-yellow *A. flavum*, with flowers like a cascading rocket. A pretty rosy-purple version of this is *A. cernuum*.

Change the water of the larger varieties regularly to minimize their oniony smell.

Alliums are easy to grow in an open, sunny situation with good drainage. Plant generous quantities in the autumn, 13cm/5in deep. When left undisturbed, most alliums will quickly form clumps. These can be divided: the spring-flowering varieties in late summer, the summer-flowering forms in spring. Alliums can be grown from seed – most will self-seed all over the garden, and some can become quite a menace, so be careful where you put them.

JUNE

- -

- -

- -

- -

- -

- -

- -

- -

- -

- -

- -

- -

- -

ROSA *Rose*

Deciduous and semi-evergreen shrub and climber

ZONES: 6–10 except: *R.* 'Cardinal de Richelieu', *R.* 'Charles de Mills', *R. gallica* 'Versicolor', *R.* 'Geranium', *R.* 'Nevada', *R.* 'Nuits de Young', *R.* 'Tuscany Superb', *R. xanthina* 'Canary Bird' 5–9; *R. glauca* 4–9; *R. mulliganii* 5–10; *R.* 'Souvenir du Docteur Jamain', 6–9

HEIGHT AND SPREAD: *R.* 'Iceberg' 90cm/3ft x 60cm/2ft; *R.* 'Cardinal de Richelieu', *R.* 'Charles de Mills', *R.* 'Felicia', *R. gallica* 'Versicolor', *R.* 'Graham Thomas', *R.* 'Heritage', *R.* 'Nuits de Young', *R.* 'Tuscany Superb' 1.2m/4ft x 1.2m/4ft; *R.* 'Fritz Nobis' 1.5m/5ft x 1.2m/4ft; *R. glauca*; *R.* 'Nevada', *R. xanthina* 'Canary Bird', *R.* 'Geranium' 2.5m/8ft x 1.8m/6ft, *R.* 'New Dawn', *R.* 'Souvenir du Docteur Jamain' 3m/10ft x 2.5m/8ft; *R. mulliganii* 4.5m/15ft x 3m/10ft

VARIETIES GOOD FOR CUTTING

Choose roses that are irresistible to you on grounds of colour or scent, but check that they will last in water. I would choose any of the deep rich chocolate-crimsons or deep purples, such as *R.* 'Cardinal de Richelieu', or even better those with golden-yellow centres and enveloping perfume, such as *R.* 'Nuits de Young' or *R.* 'Tuscany Superb', which has the colour and texture of the most luxurious silk-velvet, gold-leaf brocaded curtain. Also, grow a rich deep pink rose such as the vibrant, intense *R.* 'Charles de Mills'. *R.* 'Fritz Nobis' is another sumptuous rose, with more open flowers and less dense petals. I have a passion for the old-fashioned, striped, bicoloured roses. Rosa mundi (*R. gallica* 'Versicolor'), the oldest, with its carmine and pink dapples and stripes, is excellent for cutting.

Arrange any of these on their own in a shallow rose bowl, with a pin-holder for support, or combine them with other regal,

velvet beauties. Choose, too, some easy-to-grow, good hard-working, scented roses which will flower over long periods. Widely known, though much maligned, pure white *R.* 'Iceberg' is a superb, productive rose. It will flower from summer to winter, with perhaps a flower or two for picking on Christmas Day. There are three pale pink roses – *R.* 'New Dawn', *R.* 'Felicia' and the modern English *R.* 'Heritage' – which fit into this category, too. They all pick well, flower from early summer until the first frosts, require minimal care and have good scent. For a similar hard-working, yellow rose, try the modern English rose *R.* 'Graham Thomas'. *R.* 'Souvenir du Docteur Jamain' is another good 'doer', and one of the most sumptuous in colour and scent. It will flower for many months, well into the autumn.

If you have room, grow a vigorous early flowering rose for spring picking. The cream *R.* 'Nevada' and primrose-yellow *R. xanthina*

'Canary Bird' will both be in flower by mid- to late spring and are rampant enough to take some heavy picking. Fill a jug with several twisting and turning boughs and place it at the centre of a large table. They will only last a few days but are lovely while they do.

If you have a wall or pergola, think of growing one of the summer-flowering, single Rambler roses. *R. mulliganii*, with its yellow buds and simple, white flowers, is ideal and not too rampant. In autumn *R.* 'Geranium' and *R. glauca* are both excellent to cut for their elegant hips.

CONDITIONING

Always cut the stem ends of roses at a sharp angle, revealing more of the pithy stem centre that absorbs water. This increases the surface area for drinking. Plunge the cut ends in boiling water for twenty seconds, before giving them a long drink in tepid water.

CULTIVATION

All the roses named above are easy to grow and will tolerate even the poorest soil. Most prefer full sun, and all like a moist but well-drained position. If you buy bare-rooted plants, ensure that you dig a hole large enough to accommodate all the roots without cramping. Place the bush in the hole, with the union (the point where the shoots join the rootstock) about 2.5cm/1in below the soil level. Replace the soil in two or three stages, shaking it down and treading firmly with the heel each time. Topdress with bonemeal. Do not plant where roses have been grown before, or you may have problems with Specific Replant Disease.

Feed in late winter or early spring with a balanced fertilizer, and apply a mulch of manure. Roses will benefit from a monthly feed during spring and summer. Deadhead repeat-flowerers. Propagate by semi-ripe cuttings in summer or hardwood cuttings in winter.

(Left to right) *Rosa* 'Iceberg', *R.* 'Charles de Mills', *R.* 'Fritz Nobis', *R. gallica* 'Versicolor', *R.* 'Nuits de Young'

JUNE

DIGITALIS
Foxglove

Biennial and perennial, some evergreen

ZONES: 4-8
HEIGHT: *D. grandiflora* 75cm/2$^{1}/_{2}$ft;
D. purpurea varieties 0.9-1.5m/3-5ft

Much as I love *D. purpurea*, the biennial wild foxglove, I find its plum-pink a harsh and difficult colour to combine with other flowers, but there are many other stately foxglove species and cultivars that are perfect for cutting. Best of all is the pure white *D.p.* f. *albiflora*, with its great spikes of massed, hanging bells, for an all-white virginal piece. Cut it short and use its soft, velvety texture to complement deep crimson and claret snapdragons, stocks and sweet Williams, as well as blue thistles, anchusas and viper's bugloss. Or mix *D.p.* f. *albiflora* with spikes from *D.p.* Excelsior Group. The smaller and finer yellow perennial *D. grandiflora*, is also good cut.

Digitalis purpurea
f. *albiflora*

LILIUM
Lily

Bulb

ZONES: 4-8
HEIGHT: *L. monadelphum* 0.5-2m/1$^{1}/_{2}$-6ft;
L. 'Fire King', *L. longiflorum* 90cm/3ft; *L.* 'Casa
Blanca', *L.* Pink Perfection Group, *L. regale*
1.2-1.5m/4-5ft

For a heady and luxurious treat there is little to beat the pure white 'Casa Blanca' lily. Its huge, open blooms, with crinkle-edged petals and burnt-brick-red pollen, exude a sumptuous, room-filling scent, and look best contrasted with stark, lichen-covered branches to highlight their beauty. *L. regale*, with its alternating deep pink and white outside petals, exudes a perfume to wake Sleeping Beauty. When cutting, leave enough stem and foliage to allow for photosynthesis. Strip the anthers from the stamens to prevent the pollen from staining your clothes.

(Left to right)
Lilium 'Casa
Blanca', *L. regale*

99

PROJECT FOR JUNE:

THE CORN SHEAF

For the main table decoration,
I can't think of anything nicer than
the colourful, simple and fresh sheaf
of bright poppies, grasses, oats and
wheat tied simply with hop-bine.

EQUIPMENT
- hop-bine (*Humulus lupulus*) or twine

PLANTS
- 30–40 corn poppies (*Papaver rhoeas*)
  and Iceland poppies (*P. nudicaule*), cut
  slightly shorter and to different lengths
- mixed wild grasses, wheat and wild
  oats, 45–60cm/18–24in long
- 10–15 alchemilla (*A. mollis*),
  30–45cm/12–18in long
- 20 cornflowers (*Centaurea cyanus*),
  45cm/18in long
- 10–15 love-in-a-mist (*N. damascena*),
  30–45cm/12–18in long

METHOD

The sheaf is too big to hold in your hand all at once, so I make up four bunches and tie them together.

Sear the stem ends of the poppies and do not recut them. For each bunch, take a handful of the mixed grasses, hold them halfway along their stems and tie together loosely with hop-bine or twine. Holding the bunch in one hand, poke in the flowers, all facing more or less the same way: the alchemilla, cornflowers and love-in-a-mist, and lastly the poppies. Place some poppies high and some low – but their stems should not reach to the bottom of the sheaf.

Tie the bunches together securely with the hop-bine or twine. Trim the stem ends (except for the poppies) so that they reach a common level.

Stand the sheaf on the table with the stems splayed slightly so that it stays upright. You can keep the flowers fresh by standing the sheaf in a little water; take it out and dry the stem ends when the table is laid. Scatter poppy petals among the plates.

JOBS FOR JUNE

WATERING AND FEEDING

- Regular and generous watering and feeding is a must in an intensively planted and productive cutting garden.

- Water at the beginning or the end of the day, or you will lose a lot of the benefit through evaporation.

- Water plants that are prone to mildew, such as delphiniums, asters, phlox and roses, in the morning.

- Give your garden a good drenching three times a week, rather than a half-hearted sprinkle every day.

- Help your annuals along with regular top-feeding.

SOWING AND PLANTING OUT BIENNIALS

- If you have not already done it, biennials such as sweet rocket, wallflowers and Iceland poppies like to be sown direct into the open ground in summer.

- Plant out spring-sown biennials such as sweet Williams and white foxgloves in lines in a prepared bed to mature during the summer.

PLANTING BULBS AND CORMS AND IRIS RHIZOMES

- You can still plant autumn-flowering bulbs and corms in early summer.

- Plant spring-flowering bulbs, such as narcissi, cyclamen, erythroniums, scillas and chionodoxas, so they can benefit from an extra two or three months in the ground.

- Divide and replant Bearded iris. This queen of the cutting garden is unusual in preferring a summer division. After flowering, dig up the rhizomes and discard the leafless centre. Trim the ends, roots and leaves and replant the new rhizome on or just below the surface facing the sun, so that it ripens to flower the following summer.

WEEDING

- Weed often; in early summer, with everything growing for all it's worth, weeds left for a week or two can easily get the better of a cutting garden.

- Remove annuals such as groundsel, speedwell, chickweed, fat hen and goose grass as soon as you see them.

- Deal with any perennial weeds such as couch grass, bindweed and ground elder by spot treatment.

JUNE

JULY

CREATING ARRANGEMENTS

Making beautiful and impressive flower arrangements is not that difficult. There are no hard and fast rules that must be slavishly obeyed. However, there are a few basic guidelines that work for me, although I sometimes disregard them deliberately when the occasion or plant demands it. Even when you bear the following advice in mind, it is important to use your imagination and follow your own inclinations.

Avoid strict symmetry at all costs

Neat domes of flowers usually look boringly restrained and predictable. Create a livelier arrangement by allowing branches to burst out in different directions, balancing an upward spike here with a downward bough of berries there. To emphasize this, use odd numbers of the dominanting flowers and spikes of foliage. Work in threes, fives and sevens, not squarely placed fours, sixes and eights. Use, for example, three of your most glamorous flower, five of your middle-sized flower and nine or eleven of a more abundant 'padding' flower.

Create a broken silhouette and a billowy effect

Don't cut everything with equal length stems. As you place your flowers, push some right into the heart of the arrangement, leaving others standing proud.

It is painful to see beautiful plants poked into a vase with no room for their natural lines, twists and turns. In general, try to allow each stem to stand or hang as it would on the parent plant in the garden. Avoid creating any vertical and horizontal lines with the dominant flower, because this will segment the vase into zones and destroy the overall effect.

Arrange in three dimensions

Even if you are making an arrangement that is to sit against a wall or window, always aim to construct it 'in the round'. Don't fall into the short-at-the-front-and-tall-in-the-back trap. It is tempting to put all your best flowers where they will be most obviously seen. But doing this will not only give your arrangement an unnatural, two-dimensional look, but also cause it to become unbalanced in weight, making it all too easy for it to topple over. If you arrange a vase that could be viewed at any angle, it will immediately look much livelier. And you will be surprised to find that you will be able to see all your flowers. Glimpsing them from varying viewpoints will make the arrangment far more dynamic.

Teaming flowers and foliage

It is usually best to team strong foliage with strong flowers and light, fluffy foliage with more delicate flowers. Each enhances the other. Robust, architectural foliage, such as acanthus, green globe artichokes or horse chestnut buds, will reinforce the flamboyant effect of flowers such as Parrot tulips, sunflowers and dahlias. If you want to soften the effect of flowers with strongly defined shapes, use feathery foliage such as dill.

Choosing foliage

Your selection of foliage or 'greenery' is as important as your choice of flowers. Even when it is used as a background, it can dictate the basic overall flavour of an arrangement. I tend to avoid the heavy dark evergreen forms of privet, box and laurel.

Emphasizing the effect of strong flowers

When yellow and brick-red sunflowers are mixed with substantial, bursting globe artichoke buds the arrangement becomes even more commanding, the focal point of a room.

Diffusing the effect of strong flowers

The impact of the same yellow and red sunflowers is softened by the feathery heads of dill, making a less powerful arrangement, one that can blend into the background.

I think that their ramrod stems can be limiting and that their glossy texture and dark tone weigh down an arrangement and tend to swamp the colour and light produced by the flowers. I choose enlivening acid-green at any opportunity and rarely make an arrangement without euphorbia or smyrnium in spring, and alchemilla, bupleurum or dill in summer and autumn.

In addition to foliage, try and forage something – pussy willow, hazel catkins, emerging spring leaves, ears of wheat, bulrushes, clematis seed heads, sprays of blackberries or crabapples – from the wilder parts of the garden. Often one of these less obvious plants can be the making of an arrangement.

Colour contrast

An arrangement is always more interesting for using at least two contrasting colours. Think of this when choosing foliage as well as flowers. If you cut some sumptuous carmine snapdragons and cosmos they could look sombre on their own, being so closely matched in colour, especially when they are teamed with one type of foliage. Adding a few deep blue salvias and gentians would immediately make the arrangement come alive. Adding acid-green and deep crimson foliage, such as dill, bupleurum and cotinus, brings richer colours and greater interest. Don't be tempted to overegg the mixture. If you go on and add two or three more flower shapes and colours, the style and grace of the arrangement may collapse.

I feel that you can successfully have either limitless colour or infinite flower variety, but not both at once. When a colour jamboree is what's wanted, it is probably better to restrict the number of types of flowers. When the flower types are limited, anything goes.

Subdued colour

The colour match between cosmos and snapdragons is almost too perfect and, with only privet foliage, there is not enough going on to arrest the eye.

Balanced colour

With blue (salvia and gentian), acid-green (dill and bupleurum) and deep purple foliage (cotinus), the arrangement immediately becomes livelier.

Chaotic colour

With yet more colours and types of flowers (here, purple lisianthus, yellow rudbeckia and white cosmos) an arrangement can become so busy that it loses its presence.

JULY

CREATING A MIXED ARRANGEMENT

1 Start with the background foliage

Use your leafiest, bulkiest foliage to create the overall basic structure.

Too dense

These branches of acorns have not been thinned and the stems have been cut to equal lengths, and placed neatly and too symmetrically, making the arrangement look dense and boring.

2 Add more background greenery

Choose something that will contrast with the fairly dark, solid shapes of the oak leaves. Fill out the arrangement to the point where you feel it could almost be left without the flowers.

Too crowded

The usually pretty bupleurum is lost in the dense green sea of leaves. The silhouette remains too solid, adding little interest to the arrangement.

Perfectly arranged

Many leaves have been removed to emphasize the acorns and lighten the effect of dark foliage. The stems are arranged so that one leans over the vase on one side, and another curves into the air on the other. The result is asymmetrical and natural.

Perfectly arranged

Strong foliage with boughs of crabapples and green love-lies-bleeding (Amaranthus caudatus) with its long, lime-green, dangly tassels contribute subtle colour contrast, as well as different shapes and textures.

3 Add the most dominant flowers

Place flowers at very different levels, some cut quite short for the heart of the arrangement, and others standing right out, left long to break up the silhouette. Avoid overpacking, so the plants can follow their natural lines and are not held too upright and alert.

Too symmetrical

An even number of flowers has been placed symmetrically in the vase. Each one is forced too far into the foliage. The result looks cramped and suffocated.

Perfectly arranged

An odd number of sunflowers has been added, all at different levels in the arrangement. The effect is open and relaxed.

AMMI MAJUS
Bishop's flower

Hardy annual
HEIGHT: 60–120cm/2–4ft

VARIETIES GOOD FOR CUTTING

Bishop's flower is the florist's cow parsley. Like Solomon's seal or guelder rose, its tall, lacy flowers transform any bunch into a light and airy arrangement. When cut short, it mixes with love-in-a-mist, cornflowers, sweet peas, snapdragons and poppies. It is also a beauty when arranged on its own – 10–15 stems cut to their full length in a waisted glass vase for the centre of a large table. Use it, too, in stylish, yet simple pompons for a summer party. Cut the stems to 30–45cm/ 12–18in to cover oasis globes to hang in a series from the ceiling.

CONDITIONING

Strip all the bottom leaves and some of the higher ones since they will yellow way before the flowers begin to age.

CULTIVATION

This is an easy plant to grow in full sun. It needs plenty of water and will flower for many weeks if it is regularly picked and not allowed to run to seed. For 0.9–1.2m/3–4ft plants, sow in autumn directly into the flowering position. The plants overwinter well and you will have flowers to pick by late spring. For smaller plants, sow in the flowering site in mid-spring. Bishop's flower self-seeds freely so transplant the seedlings into beds or rows.

Ammi majus

ANETHUM GRAVEOLENS
Dill

Hardy annual

HEIGHT: 60–150cm/2–5ft

VARIETIES GOOD FOR CUTTING

Grow dill in as large a quantity as space allows. It is an elegant and striking filler in the garden, and invaluable in any bunch of flowers. The tiny individual florets combine into light and fluffy, yellow-green umbrellas, which give a lift to any arrangement. Mix it, as your primary foliage, with startling oranges and blues, with whites and greens, or best of all as a stark contrast to the rich Venetian colours of carmine, crimson, purple and lapis lazuli.

CONDITIONING

Strip all but the top leaves, and plunge the cut stem ends into boiling water for twenty seconds. It will then last for about ten days in water.

CULTIVATION

Plant small plants or seed plugs 20–25cm/8–10in apart. Dill will thrive in any poor, well-drained soil in full sun, as long as you water the plants in well initially, and keep them moist and well weeded until they become established. Cutting and watering make for bushy, vigorous plants, and prevent them going to seed, but will exhaust them in the end. Repeat sowings or plantings, every 3–4 weeks, are needed for a good supply. Sow seed *in situ* in thick lines or blocks in the garden. The seeds are large, so can be placed individually in the drills before being covered with soil. Thin to 20–25cm/8–10in apart in each direction, and provide some support using canes. For early flowers, sow under cover in early spring, using pots or plug trays (do not sow into seed trays because dill does not like being transplanted). Space the seed evenly in your pot, or sow four per plug, and then cover them with perlite. Germination takes 2–4 weeks. Plant out when the risk of frost has passed. Dill is another promiscuous self-seeder and can become a menace. If you fail to pick the flower heads for the house, you should cut them down before the seeds ripen and disperse. Keep dill and fennel well apart, or they will cross-pollinate.

Anethum graveolens

113

DIANTHUS
Pink, Carnation, Sweet William

Annual, biennial and perennial

ZONES: 4–8
HEIGHT: old-fashioned and laced pinks,
modern hybrids 23–30cm/9–12in;
D. caryophyllus, D. chinensis 25–35cm/10–14in;
D. barbatus 45cm/18in

Sweet Williams (*D. barbatus*) are the first to
bloom. Grow them in jolly coloured panels
of pink, white and crimson, single and
bicoloured mixtures, with single or double
flowers, or in groups of single colours.
Of the biennial kinds, there is the small-
flowered, highly scented, almost black *D.b.*
Nigrescens Group. Grow also a rich crimson
variety, best just plain with no white eye, such
as *D.b.* 'Dunnet's Dark Crimson', and pure
white *D.b.* 'Albus'. Cut tall, use the deep rich
reds in fragrant combinations of claret stocks
and snapdragons, contrasted with deep
blue anchusas. Use *D.b.* Nigrescens Group
in a bedside bunch of sweet peas and roses.
Recently developed annual forms of sweet
Williams will guarantee you flowers in the
same year from a late winter sowing. From
the huge range of perennial hybrid pinks
choose the taller, larger varieties. Two of my
favourites are the double-flowered, pale pink
D. 'Alice' and the rich crimson, pink-edged
D. 'Laced Monarch'.

(Left to right) *Dianthus barbatus*
Nigrescens Group, *D.* 'Alice',
D. 'Laced Monarch'

JULY

JULY

ANTIRRHINUM
Snapdragon

Perennial and semi-evergreen subshrub, usually grown as an annual

ZONES: 5–9
HEIGHT: dwarf cultivars (e.g. *A. majus* 'Black Prince') 45cm/18in; tall cultivars (e.g. *A.* Forerunner Series) 90cm/36in

Nurseries and garden centres sell trays of snapdragons, but they are usually of mixed colours. It is better to sow your own. Treat them as half-hardy annuals and sow under glass or in a propagator in late winter. Don't pinch out the leaders of your seedlings if you want a nice tall stem for cutting. Plant out into pre-fed ground when the risk of frost is over: snapdragons need sun and rich, well-drained soil. Plant closer than the seed packet directs so that a little competition for light helps the plants to maximize their height. Water and pick snapdragons regularly, and they will go on flowering well into autumn.

Antirrhinum majus 'Liberty Crimson', *A.m.* 'White Wonder'

EREMURUS
Foxtail lily, King's spear

Bulbous perennial

ZONES: *E. himalaicus* 3–9; *E. robustus*, Ruiter Hybrid 6–9; *E. stenophyllus* 5–9
HEIGHT: *E. stenophyllus* 0.9–1.2m/3–4ft; Ruiter Hybrid 1.5m/5ft; *E. himalaicus*, *E. robustus* 1.8–2.5m/6–8ft

These tapering, towering spikes of small, starry flowers look more like the tail feathers of a giant exotic jungle parrot than a fox's brush – you can imagine them trailing down from a high branch of a mahogony tree, entirely surrounded by orchids and ferns, and humid, mossy smells. They make luxurious and opulent cut flowers in white, cream, pink, orange and bright yellow. Mix them in any great summer arrangement, or have them on their own, the colours jumbled like a collection of coloured sparklers.

(Left to right)
Eremurus stenophyllus,
E. × *isabellinus* Ruiter
Hybrid

117

PROJECT FOR JULY:

SUMMER ABUNDANCE

This sumptuous celebration of summer is worthy of a still-life painting. Here for the picking are flowers of unsurpassed stature and opulence. Go over the top in creating this one, with huge alliums and agapanthus, great wands of eremurus and delphiniums and heavy-headed, heady-scented lilies.

EQUIPMENT
• china urn, 45–60cm/18–24in tall

PLANTS
5–9 stems of each of the following, using as much height as possible:
• eremurus (*E. stenophyllus*)
• delphiniums (*D.* 'Cristella' or *D.* 'Nobility')
• eryngiums (*E. alpinum* 'Amethyst')
• dill (*Anethum graveolens*)
• bells of Ireland (*Moluccella laevis*)
• alliums (*A. giganteum*)
• lupins (*Lupinus* 'The Governor')
• lilies (*Lilium* 'Casa Blanca')
• orange pot marigolds (*Calendula officinalis* Art Shades Group)
• agapanthus (*A. campanulatus* var. *albidus*)

METHOD
First position the dominant structural flowers, the eremurus and the delphiniums, to give the arrangement its height and architecture. Make sure they are placed asymmetrically.

Add the eryngiums, green dill and bells of Ireland. Put in the alliums, the lupins and the lilies next, placing them some high and some lower, and giving emphasis to the centre rather than the silhouette. Use the bright, contrasting pot marigolds to punctuate the centre.

Finally, position the towering stems of agapanthus, using them to break up any neat lines and unbalance any symmetry that may have crept in as you placed the other flowers.

PLANTING OUT LATE-FLOWERING ANNUALS

- As your wallflowers, Iceland poppies, sweet Williams and sweet peas come to an end, fill the gaps with later flowers nurtured in the cold frame, such as *Nicotiana sylvestris*, rudbeckias, zinnias, tithonia, amaranthus and *Euphorbia marginata*. Remove the spent plants, feed the soil and plant out.

- Harvest hardy annual seed at this time of year, such as cerinthe and pot marigolds. From a spring sowing, they'll be going over now and dropping seed where they grow. Before it's all dispersed, pick whole plants and tie them upside down in a pillowcase and allow the seeds to drop out. They'll continue to dry in the air-permeable cotton, ready for you when you want to autumn sow.

JULY

AUGUST

TAKING SEMI-RIPE CUTTINGS

If you want to build up a good clump of a favourite plant, or if you are thinking of lining a path in the garden with lavender or rosemary, late summer is the time to take your semi-ripe cuttings.

- Pamper a strong, healthy plant to use for taking cuttings. It is worth giving a chosen plant plenty of food and water so that it is ready, with lots of new growth, when you want to take cuttings.

- Remove the whole shoot from the parent plant by pulling or cutting it off at the junction with the main branch.
- Take more cuttings than you need, and store them immediately in a closed plastic bag to minimize water loss. Pot them up as soon as possible, and take out no more than two at a time.
- Label each pot with the name of the plant and the date.
- You can fit several cuttings in a pot as long as they don't touch.

Propagating with semi-ripe cuttings

1 *Set out the equipment you need: labels, 8–10cm/3–4in square plastic pots, hormone rooting powder, a bowl of water, secateurs, a sharp knife, a dibber, plastic bags, short canes or sticks, rubber bands and a watering can. Have one bucket of compost (loam, peat and sand mixed with a slow-release fertilizer) and one of vermiculite or sharp sand. In the third bucket, make a well-draining mix of one-third vermiculite to two-thirds compost. Fill the pots with this mix.*

2 *Cut or pull healthy, non-flowering, 8–10cm/3–4in long side shoots from the parent plant. Gather the cuttings in a plastic bag. At the workbench, remove leaves and side shoots from the lower two-thirds of the stem. Pinch out the soft tip. Make a neat cut at an angle just beneath this year's new wood. Dip the stem end in water, then into the hormone rooting powder, and tap off any excess. Use a dibber to make a hole in the vermiculite/compost mix and push the cutting in to about one-third its length. Firm the compost and water well.*

- Cover each pot with a plastic bag, to retain moisture. But do not let the cuttings come into contact with the plastic. If this happens, mildew may well set in.
- Check cuttings and water them regularly. Remove any cuttings that show signs of wilt, disease or mildew. They will infect others.

4 *After two weeks to a month, turn one pot out to see if good strong roots have formed. If so, it is time to pot the rooted cuttings up individually in fresh, moist vermiculte/compost mix. Make a hole in the fresh compost with your fingers. Plant the rooted cuttings and firm in. Water to dislodge any air pockets.*

5 *Replace the cuttings on the propagator bench or windowsill, without plastic bags, for another 2–3 weeks. Then move to a cold frame or a cooler spot until ready to plant up in spring.*

3 *Place canes in each corner of the pot and stretch a plastic bag over, secured with a rubber band, to make a moisture-retaining tent. Position the cuttings on a propagator bench or on a warm windowsill, but out of bright sunlight. Alternatively, put the pots in a mist propagator.*

COSMOS

**Half-hardy annual and
tuberous perennial**

ZONES: *C. atrosanguineus* 8–9
HEIGHT AND SPREAD: *C. atrosanguineus*
60cm/2ft; *C. bipinnatus* 1.2m/4ft

(Left to right) *Cosmos atrosanguineus,
C. bipinnatus* 'Purity', *C.b.* 'Versailles
Carmine'

VARIETIES GOOD
FOR CUTTING

The annual cosmos is definitely among the
plants that best earn their keep in the cutting
garden. These tall, bushy annuals flower and
flower, providing cut flowers of sumptuous
colours and fragile texture from late spring
until the first hard frosts. Grow *C. bipinnatus*
'Purity', whose crinkled, saucer-shaped
flowers mix with everything, and the deep
carmine-pink *C.b.* 'Dazzler'. Put them on
their own in a jug on a windowsill, where
their thin petals will catch the light.

From late summer through autumn,
the deep claret-crimson, tender perennial
C. atrosanguineus, the chocolate-smelling
cosmos, comes into flower.

CONDITIONING

Give these robust, long-lasting flowers a
good cool drink.

CULTIVATION

Cosmos like full sun and moist but well-
drained soil. The annuals thrive with regular
topdressing, watering and picking. In mild
areas, tubers of half-hardy *C. atrosanguineus*
may be overwintered in the ground if
protected with a deep mulch. In more
severe climates, lift them and store as for
tender tubers. Start them into growth in the
greenhouse and plant out in early summer.

Propagate annuals from seed in early
spring. Sow under cover, with some heat.
Prick them out when they are large enough
to handle, and gradually reduce the heat.
Transfer to cold frames and plant out
when all risk of frost has gone. Propagate
C. atrosanguineus from basal cuttings in spring
or from semi-ripe cuttings in late summer.

ACANTHUS
Bear's breeches

Semi-evergreen herbaceous perennial

ZONES: *A. hungaricus* 6–10,
A. mollis 8–10; *A. spinosus*
HEIGHT: 0.9–1.5m/3–5ft;
A. spinosus to 1.8m/6ft

VARIETIES GOOD FOR CUTTING

The imposing, foxglove-like flower spikes of acanthus are a mixture of green, purple, white and pink, each clad in 20–30 flowers. Mix them with other strong and structural flowers such as sunflowers and cardoons, or arrange many stems on their own. For the greatest number of flower spikes choose *A. spinosus*, although *A. hungaricus* is also free-flowering. *A. mollis* and *A. spinosus* Spinosissimus Group, whose elegant, finely divided foliage is an asset in any garden, produce fewer flowers.

CONDITIONING

Beware of the long, sharp spikes in the flowers when cutting and arranging. Plunge the stem ends into boiling water for twenty seconds; the flowers will then last up to two weeks in water.

CULTIVATION

Plant acanthus in groups of three or five in spring, and protect the crowns with a mulch in the first winter. They may take a year or two to settle in and start flowering, so be patient. Acanthus will grow in shade, but for lots of flower spikes choose a site with deep, well-drained, fertile soil in full sun, where its roots can bake. They can become invasive and, once established, their long, thong-like roots are difficult to eradicate. Propagate acanthus from root cuttings in winter or by division in autumn or early spring.

Acanthus mollis

127

HELIANTHUS
Sunflower

Hardy annual
HEIGHT: 1–3m/3–10ft

VARIETIES GOOD FOR CUTTING

The open, generous, cheery faces of the annuals, *H. annuus*, come in all shades of yellow, cream and now rich maroon and mahogany. As a bonus, the petals often contrast with a lovely, chocolatey centre, matching the bumblebees that crawl all over them. If picked in bud or recently opened, the flowers will last in water, looking fresh and succulent, for more than two weeks. Grow the new empress of sunflowers *H.a.* 'Velvet Queen', the pale yellow *H.a.* 'Lemon Queen' and some of the classic bright golden-yellow forms, such as *H.a.* 'Henry Wilde' and *H.a.* 'Valentine', and try too some of the multicoloured cream, yellow, orange, crimson and mahogany mixtures.

CONDITIONING

Put straight into water and keep stems away from heat.

CULTIVATION

Plant 6–8 plants per square metre/yard, in full sun, in moist but well-drained soil. They will tolerate light shade, but remember that the flowers will always face the sun. Provide support, because the wind may catch the giant heavy heads.

Sow sunflowers directly into their flowering position in the spring. Place the large, flat seeds in groups in the border, or in lines in the cutting patch. Keep them well watered. Or sow early under cover in individual pots in a propagator or greenhouse, planting them out when the risk of frost is over.

(Left to right) *Helianthus annuus* 'Henry Wilde', *H.a.* 'Velvet Queen'

128

AUGUST

AUGUST

ZINNIA

Half-hardy annual

HEIGHT: 30-90cm/12-36in

VARIETIES GOOD FOR CUTTING

This huge family ranges from Las Vegas to Venetian silks, from Manhattan blare to Old World richness. I love all of them, but the very best is the double, lime-green *Z*. 'Envy'. Mix it with contrasting deep crimsons and reds, or arrange one or two stems simply on their own, to appreciate its exquisite and dramatic but calming colour. For reds and oranges choose from *Z. elegans* Cactus-flowered Group and *Z*. Scabiosa-flowered Group.

CONDITIONING

Just strip the bottom leaves. These long-lived cut flowers should look good for at least two weeks.

CULTIVATION

Plant zinnias out in full sun in fertile, well-drained soil. Pick them regularly from the moment they start flowering and they will continue to flower until winter. They do best in baking hot summers, but take care not to overwater them once they are in the ground; they can suffer from mildew. Propagate from seed sown under cover in late spring. Prick the seedlings out and pot them up, taking care not to overwater.

(Left to right) *Zinnia* Scabiosa-flowered Group, *Z*. 'Envy', *Z. elegans* Cactus-flowered Group

AGAPANTHUS
African lily

Perennial, some evergreen

ZONE: 8–10; *A.* Headbourne Hybrids 6–9
HEIGHT: most are 60–150cm/2–5ft

VARIETIES GOOD FOR CUTTING

These many-flowered, blue pompons on their king
straight stalks look like maces in an ecclesiastical
procession. Arrange them in tall, narrow vases on
their own, or combine them, in an explosion of flower
colour, with eremurus and alliums. Grow the hardiest,
A. Headbourne Hybrids, which come in a range of colours
from deep blue to white. For the tall and stately, choose
mid-blue *A.* 'Loch Hope', with its flower spikes of 1.5m/5ft.
A. 'Buckingham Palace' is a richer blue and even taller, but
with a less generous number of flowers. Of the smaller
varieties to mix with roses, phlox and bupleurum, try dark
blue *A.* 'Lilliput', which stands only 30cm/12in high. The
paler-coloured, deciduous *A. campanulatus* varieties are almost
completely hardy, too. Look out for the hardiest of all, *A.c.*
subsp. *patens* and handsome *A.c.* var. *albidus*. The angular
agapanthus seed heads are lovely in autumn arrangements.

CONDITIONING

Pick when there are still many unopened flowers, and
remove dead florets as they age.

CULTIVATION

To get the best midnight-blue varieties, choose your
agapanthus plants when in flower. Plant generous clumps
of 3–5, depending on their size. These are sun-loving plants
which thrive in fertile soil that is moist but well drained,
particularly during the winter months. They will do best
with the shelter of a sunny wall. Protect the crowns in
winter with a good layer of mulch. Clumps increase slowly,
but after some years can be divided in the spring.

(Left to right) *Agapanthus* 'Loch
Hope', *A. campanulatus* var. *albidus*

AUGUST

PROJECT FOR AUGUST:

COLLECTION OF SCARLETS AND BLUES

The velvety textures and rich colours of the scarlet lychnis, green tobacco plants and purple-blue anchusas and alliums contrast well with the clear simplicity of the blue- and grey-striped jug. The single zinnia in its blue glass continues the theme. Flowers often look more beautiful grouped in a collection of vases, decanters and jugs like this than they would if simply standing on their own.

EQUIPMENT
• blue china jug
• jug, 30cm/12in tall

PLANTS
5–7 stems, 45–60cm/18–24in long, of each of the following:
• anchusas (*A. azurea*)
• salvias (*S. patens* and *S.* x *superba*)
• tobacco plants (*Nicotiana* 'Lime Green')
• alliums (*A. cernuum, A. neapolitanum* Cowanii Group, *A. sphaerocephalon*)
• triteleia (*T. laxa* 'Koningin Fabiola')
• lychnis (*L. chalcedonica* and *L.* x *arkwrightii* 'Vesuvius')
• orange alstroemerias (*A. ligtu* hybrids)
• globe artichokes (*Cynara cardunculus* Scolymus Group)
• a single zinnia (*Z.* 'Envy')

METHOD
For this arrangement, place the flowers first and the artichoke foliage last. Using the robust anchusas and salvias, make a structure about 1½ times the height of the jug. Their stems make a network into which you can add the tobacco plants, the alliums and the triteleia, to create an up and down rhythm in the bunch.

Add the contrasting bright lychnis and alstroemerias before placing the artichokes. Put some artichoke foliage at the heart of the arrangement and some right on the edge.

Place the single, green zinnia in the blue glass to highlight the acid-green colour scattered among the flowers.

PICKING AND DEADHEADING

- Keep picking, deadheading and removing seed cases to prolong the flowering season. Delphiniums, foxgloves and other perennials will develop lateral flower buds when you remove the leader, and violas will flower for many months if their seed cases are removed. Repeat-flowering roses such as *Rosa* 'New Dawn', *R*. 'Felicia' and *R*. 'Iceberg' will bear new flowering shoots if you cut stems back to a vigorous shooting bud.

Rosa 'Felicia'

AUGUST

SEPTEMBER

GROWING IN THE MIXED GARDEN

If you have no separate area to devote to cut flowers, think of making some space in different parts of your garden so that you can grow a range of plants for cutting. The least you will need are several spots in full sun, a few in shadier positions, an area for climbers and somewhere to grow tall and small plants. Here is a scheme that is both productive and decorative for much of the year. It measures 9m/30ft × 12m/40ft and has a brick-paved terrace leading to French windows and the kitchen door. To maximize use, the planting scheme focuses on salads, herbs and a few vegetables, as well as flowers and foliage for the house.

THE DESIGN

This layout can be adapted to a range of needs. For example, if you wanted to include grass, the central bed could be made into a small lawn. The brick paths are wide enough to allow a wheelbarrow or children's tricycles to pass, and the beds and borders allow easy picking of the plants. The mass of plants is given order and coherence by the low clipped box hedges, the rounded box balls and pairs of mophead bay in pots that punctuate the design.

THE PLANTS THROUGH THE YEAR

Although the garden is seen here in high summer, there are lots of spring flowers planted among the shrub and perennial borders: hyacinths, tulips and anemones grouped in panels down the path, with biennial forget-me-nots and wallflowers, scillas and miniature narcissi under the old apple tree; crown imperials and Solomon's seal combine in the shady border.

The summer annuals – including pot marigolds, violas, snapdragons and love-in-a-mist – can be mixed with euphorbias, bupleurum, bells of Ireland and dill for your foliage. There are deep crimson, scented roses and pink *Rosa* 'New Dawn' and white *R.* 'Iceberg', which will flower until the severe frosts. Among the perennials are lupins, anchusas, peonies and echinops, while white and spotted foxgloves are massed beside the hedge. As long as you pick them, many of the annuals, such as tithonia and sunflowers, will flower through the autumn

The summer vegetables are selected for dwarf or ornamental characteristics that integrate well with the flowers. As well as miniature broad beans, there are green and crimson lettuces, rocket, aubergines, tomatoes, beans climbing with the sweet peas, and nasturtiums and viola flowers for adding to salads.

Sunny terrace beds

The beautiful, deep purple-blue flowers of the agapanthus growing all along this bed will later produce elegant seed heads. Deep purple-black aubergines are grown along the low wall and there is a splash of red from cherry tomatoes. The blue-purple colour theme continues into autumn with alliums and various salvias, and in winter with Iris reticulata and I. unguicularis. Green and crimson lettuces flank a large clump of alchemilla along the path, with the alchemilla repeated on both sides of the foreground steps. The small bed here has soft pink Rosa 'New Dawn' growing with tall Allium sphaerocephalon.

Shrub and perennial beds

Scrambling all along the hazel hurdle fence are clematis including the rich-coloured C. *'Étoile Violette' and* C. *'Royal Velours'. Other climbers include the purple-flowered* Akebia quinata, *as backdrop to a group of deep crimson* Rosa *'Tuscany Superb' while* Lonicera × brownii *and* Solanum crispum *'Glasnevin' are behind a ceanothus close to the terrace. The highly scented honeysuckle* Lonicera periclymenum *'Serotina' climbs through* Salix daphnoides *in the corner farthest from the house.*

The shaded beds along the hedge

Sarcococca grows on either side of the bench and lily-of-the-valley (Convallaria majalis) *beneath it. In the corner are the tall spires of white foxgloves* (Digitalis purpurea f. albiflora), *with Solomon's seal* (Polygonatum), *pulmonaria* (P. *'Sissinghurst White'), hostas and white dicentras growing in the shade of the apple tree. Beyond the tree are tall, white and blue delphiniums against claret roses, and planted between the box balls in front of* Paeonia lactiflora *'Shirley Temple' are herbs (rocket and acid-green dill), and lettuces.*

Centre beds

The wigwam is clothed in Lathyrus odoratus *'Matucana' and other varieties of sweet pea. These are mixed with the delicious, deep purple form of French climbing bean. Lining the paths of the central bed are parsley and thyme, pot marigolds, purple-green basil and lettuces. Nearer the centre are blue lupins and anchusas, feverfew, purple alliums and greenish-purple or silver eryngiums, the chocolate-brown cosmos* C. *atrosanguineus and deep crimson* Rosa *'Cardinal de Richelieu'.*

Perennial beds

A hop plant (Humulus lupulus) *climbs through a circular hazel structure with tall spikes of larkspur* (Consolida *Exquisite Series 'Blue Spire') and hairy spikes of* Anchusa azurea *'Loddon Royalist' either side. Along the path are clumps of silver-white convolvulus* (C. cneorum) *and white arctotis* (A. fastuosa *'Zulu Prince'). Pink catmint* (Nepeta) *grows with tall cerise* Lobelia cardinalis *'Queen Victoria' under the mophead bay tree. In the bed to the right, the orange-reds continue with red and gold aquilegias and red dicentra* (D. formosa *'Bacchanal').*

GLADIOLUS

Corm

ZONE: *G. communis* subsp. *byzantinus* 6–9;
Guildhall hybrids 9–10
HEIGHT AND SPREAD: 0.9m–1.5 m/3–5ft x 10–15cm/4–6in

(Left to right)
Gladiolus 'Black Lash',
G. 'Sunshine',
G. 'Purple Flora'

VARIETIES GOOD FOR CUTTING

Gladioli have had their reputation ruined by the hideous pinks, pale butterscotch-oranges and washed-out yellows that you inevitably find in funeral wreaths and floral tributes. Poor flower! There are sumptuous crimson, violet, lime-green, burnt-orange and nearly black gladiolus hybrids, not to mention the head-turning deep carmine-pink *G. communis* subsp. *byzantinus*. Look for 'Green Star', with its sulphurous-green flowers to mix with the choc-crimson, almost black 'Espresso', the lovely rich reddish purple 'Plum Tart' and the purple velvet 'Purple Flora'. One of my favourites is the claret-red 'Black Lash' – perfect when used as a strong spike with huge sunflowers, thistles and dahlias to break up the symmetry of a hanging globe.

CONDITIONING

Remove the bottom leaves. Some people cut off the top 5cm/2in of the flower spike to make sure the flowers lower down all come out; I think this a shame, as the twists and turns of the spike end are an integral part of the plant's appeal.

CULTIVATION

Choose summer-flowering gladioli when in flower, or order corms from a well-illustrated list of a good bulb wholesaler, to make sure you get the best colours. Plant them out after the last spring frosts, and stagger the planting at ten-day intervals from mid-spring to midsummer, to prolong the season. Choose a site in full sun with light soil rich in organic material. Plant them 10cm/4in deep and 10–15cm/4–6in apart in clumps or lines in the cutting garden. Water regularly and plentifully during the growing season, and stake the taller varieties. Lift your corms after the first frost, cut off their stems, dry and clean them, and rigorously discard any with signs of disease. Dust them with with fungicide and store in a frost-free, cool, airy place until the following year. Plant spring-flowerers, such as *G. communis* subsp. *byzantinus*, in autumn.

DAHLIA

Tuberous perennial
ZONE: 9
HEIGHT: 0.9m-2m/3-7ft

VARIETIES GOOD FOR CUTTING

I grow dahlias in nearly all their shapes and forms. You can grow tall, voluptuous ones such as 'Edinburgh', or jazzy, rich burnt-orange 'Happy Halloween' to mix with deep crimson 'Rip City' or almost black 'Karma Choc'. More subtle varieties are 'Bishop of Llandaff', with its scarlet petals and central ruff, and rich crimson 'Bishop of Auckland'. Both have exotic dark crimson foliage and combine effectively with lime-green *Zinnia* 'Envy'.

CONDITIONING

Only pick dahlias in fill flower. The buds tend to wither and die without opening. Recut the hollow stem ends under water to avoid airlocks.

CULTIVATION

Select tubers in flower at a good nursery, or from a reliably illustrated list; colour descriptions are always misleading. Start dahlias into growth in spring and they will have formed good plants by early summer, when you can plant them out in a sunny position in well-drained soil. Add a handful of bonemeal to the planting hole and plant the tubers 10cm/4in below the surface. When they are growing strongly, pinch out the tip of the main stem to encourage bushy growth. Stake the taller varieties. Keep the plants well watered in the summer and, if you are not picking them, deadhead them as the flowers fade. After flowering, lift the tubers and store them in a frost-free place. Propagate dahlias from basal cuttings.

(Left to right) *Dahlia* 'Arabian Night', 'Bishop of Llandaff', 'Downham Royal', 'Edinburgh'

143

SEPTEMBER

Abutilon 'Ashford Red'

COTINUS
Burning bush, Smokebush

Deciduous shrub and tree

ZONE: 5-8
HEIGHT AND SPREAD: *C. coggygria*
2.5-4m/8-13ft x 2.5-4m/8-13ft;
C. obovatus 6m/20ft x 4.5m/15ft

C. coggygria is a large plant for the average-sized cutting garden, but its summer foliage and flowers, and even better its autumnal, vibrant orange, pink, red and purple leaves, are spectacular for cutting. These are easily grown shrubs, which will thrive in any reasonably drained soil. Too fertile a soil can inhibit the development of autumn colours and make the shrubs coarse and sappy. They do best and colour most dramatically in full sun; the purple-leaved varieties tend to revert to green in shade. Prune to remove dead wood in spring. If you cut them back hard you will not get the feathery hat of summer flowers, which are produced on wood three years old or more. You will, however, gain larger leaves.

ABUTILON

Herbaceous perennial and deciduous shrub

ZONE: 9-10
HEIGHT AND SPREAD: *A.* 'Ashford Red',
A. 'Canary Bird' 0.9-1.8m/3-6ft x 45-90cm/
18-36in; *A. x sutense cultivars*,
A. vitifolium 1.8-3m/6-10ft x 90cm/3ft

With generous, open, saucer- and bell-shaped flowers in rich reds, yellows, oranges, purples and whites, abutilons make statuesque additions to any bunch and are also perfect as single stems for a desk or bedside table. Grow the more tender varieties, such as *A.* 'Ashford Red' and *A.* 'Canary Bird', in large pots so that they can be moved inside during winter. They like moist but not wet soil. Feed them well for a good, long flowering season. Cut them to the ground in winter, and they will be covered in new growth and leaves by mid-spring.

Cotinus coggygria
'Royal Purple'

145

SCHIZOSTYLIS COCCINEA

Bulb
ZONE: 8-9
HEIGHT: 60cm/24in

Pick a generous bunch of these miniature, gladiolus-like, deep pink and red flowers. The delicate flower spikes, with their neat, cup-shaped blooms held on thin stems, look best en masse. When their flowers are fully open in sun, their darker colours shine as if cut from the finest iridescent silk. These slightly tender bulbs will provide a strong splash of colour even after the first frosts have clobbered almost everything else. Grow rich scarlet-pink *S. coccinea* 'Major' or the smaller-flowered, white *S.c.* f. *alba* and salmon-pink *S.c.* 'Sunrise'.

Schizostylis coccinea 'Major'

HELENIUM
Sneezeweed

Herbacious perennial
ZONE: 4-8
HEIGHT: 0.9-1.5m/3-5ft

The petals of these big-boned, daisy-like flowers fold back from the fuzzy central hub, almost like the wings of an insect. The heleniums have an air that somehow combines the obvious with the delicate; they do everything that an aster does but more so. Plant them in full sun. They will survive in any soil short of a bog. Support the heavy flowering stems with a network of hazel sticks. The clumps quickly get congested and thrive on regular division in spring or autumn. If you buy one plant, you will soon have a good colony.

(Left to right) *Helenium* 'Butterpat', *H.* 'Moerheim Beauty'

SEPTEMBER

PROJECT FOR SEPTEMBER:

AN AUTUMN COLLECTION

By autumn there is no longer the summer abundance to choose from, so collect a few stems of many different things – whatever is still around – and arrange them by colour. None of the vases here would make an impact on its own but, when combined, each one becomes part of a sumptuous and handsome group. The hop medallion and a scattering of hop seeds on the table serve to link the different elements of the display.

EQUIPMENT
- glasses and vases of varying heights, including a thin-necked vase, e.g. a traditional hyacinth glass
- 15–20 marbles for the small vases, to hold fragile stems in place
- strong binding wire, for the base of the hop medallion

PLANTS
- hop-bine (*Humulus lupulus*)

the following flowers and foliage, cut 1½–2 times vase heights:
- 5–7 ampelopsis (*A. brevipedunculata*)
- 3–5 euonymus (*E. europaeus*)
- 3–5 abutilons (*A.* 'Ashford Red')
- 7–9 cosmos (*C. atrosanguineus*)
- 3–5 deep red violas (*Viola* variety)
- 7–9 dahlias (*D.* 'Bishop of Llandaff')
- 3–5 purple violas (*Viola* variety)
- 3–5 large-flowered nicandras (*N. physalodes*)
- 3 anchusas (*A. azurea* 'Lodden Royalist')
- 7–9 gentian heads (*Gentiana triflora*)

METHOD
Make the hop-bine medallion first (see pages 190–91). Entwine one end of hop-bine into the other and it will stay put. Arrange the ampelopsis, euonymus and abutilons in separate vases. Put the cosmos and red violas in the thin-necked vase, and the dahlias in a vase on their own. Place the purple violas, nicandras and anchusas in one small vase with the marbles and the gentian flowers in the other.

JOBS FOR SEPTEMBER

BULB CARE
AND PLANTING

- Select and plant your bulbs with their flowering dates in mind. You can then have a continuous flow of bright and brilliant flowers for many months at the beginning of the year.

- Prepare the soil before planting. Bulbs on the whole like humus-rich and very well-drained soil. Add organic matter and grit or coarse sand, according to your soil type.

- Knock tall, wooden, gloss-painted markers into the ground before planting bulbs in the cutting garden. Put one at each end of the planned row where they will stay from one year to the next, to mark exactly where your bulbs are.

- Try to plant your bulbs as soon as they arrive. With the exception of tulips, the sooner they get in the ground the better.

- Look for signs of old roots on cyclamen corms. This will tell you which way up to plant them.

- Plant anemone corms with their flat axis horizontal, but it does not seem to matter which way up you set them.

- Delay planting tulips until the really cold weather starts. Plant them with the pointed end upright.

- Do not tread the soil in after planting as this may break off the growing point of the bulb; just firm it gently with the flat of your hand.

- To naturalize bulbs in grass, cut and remove a circle of turf and use a bulb planter to remove a core of soil 5–8cm/2–3in deep. Place your bulb in the hole and replace the soil and the turf.

COLLECTING AND
PLANTING SEEDS
AND SEEDLINGS

- Seed collecting starts in summer, but most is done in autumn. To save the expense of buying annuals every year it is well worth collecting seeds from all but the F1 hybrids, which do not come true from seed.

- Catch the seed cases when they are turning brown and drying up. Pick the seed case whole and store it in a labelled paper envelope. Store them in a cool, dry place until you are ready to plant them in seed trays or in the open.

- Dig up any hardy annual, self-sown seedlings and plant them in blocks or lines.

- Put some of your hardy annual seeds, especially cornflowers and love-in-a-mist, straight into the ground. These plants mature earlier and will extend your season of flowering.

SEPTEMBER

OCTOBER

CHOOSING THE RIGHT VASE

If you marry your flowers to a vase that is sympathetic in shape and colour, you are halfway to creating a beautiful arrangement. So it is important that, when you begin to grow flowers for cutting, you should also invest in at least a basic variety of vases and containers.

I recommend the following: a simple clear glass vase, full-bellied with a neck, 20–30cm/8–12in high; a similar-shaped vase or a jug which is about 45cm/18in high, for generous, larger arrangements; a tall, straight or slightly shaped vase 20–30cm/8–12in high; a tall, narrow vase for a single rose or giant tobacco flower; at least one or two shallow ceramic or glass bowls for table centres; a few coloured glasses for smaller posies and single flower heads for putting beside a bed or on your desk, as well as one or two 2.5–5cm/1–2in vases for a single crocus or auricula. As you grow more and varied flowers, and become more adventurous in your arrangements, you will find that you want to add to your vase collection all the time.

Height of vase

For any arrangement to be in harmonious proportion, the height of the vase you choose should be one-third to one-half the height of the tallest flowers and foliage you have picked. If the vase is more than this, it will make the flowers appear as if they are straining to peep out of the top. If it is less, then the whole arrangement will look as if it is about to topple over.

Colour and style of vase

I love bright, contrasting colours and so my favourite arrangements are often those with zingy pink flowers in turquoise or apple-green ceramic or glass containers. A few stems of

crimson *Hyacinthus* 'Jan Bos', for example, will combine with a container of an equally strong but contrasting colour to produce a powerful attention-seeker. A subtle mixture of more delicate flowers, such as love-in-a-mist with cornflowers, delphiniums and alchemilla, needs a lighter, less dominant vase.

Similarly, great bosomy peonies and roses can look good in an elaborate vase, while simple, wild-style flowers on the whole look better in unpatterned, unfussy containers. It is important that the vase never overwhelms the flowers.

Acquire a good collection of vases

Choose plain glass or a neutral-coloured material such as pewter to get the most use out of your vases to begin with, but don't neglect other colours. You will soon learn which sizes, shapes and colours suit your favourite flowers and arrangements.

Stems too long

These cosmos look as if they could topple the vase over at any minute. This lack of balance is visually uncomfortable.

Stems too short

Some of these stems look as if they are having to crane their necks to reach out of the vase. Again, such disproportion is best avoided.

Stems in good proportion

These stems are 2–3 times the height of the vase, creating an arrangement that looks stable and open.

SALVIA *Sage*

Annual, tender perennial and shrub

ZONES: *S. patens* 9–10; *S. x superba* 5–9; *S. uliginosa* 8–9
HEIGHT: *S. patens, S. x superba* 75cm/30in; *S. uliginosa* to 1.5m/5ft

VARIETIES GOOD FOR CUTTING

The huge sage family, with its simple, double-lipped flowers in resonant colours and soft, tempting textures, is vital in autumn. *S. patens* includes pretty, pale blue *S.p.* 'Cambridge Blue' and pale mauve *S.p.* 'Chilcombe', which begin flowering in summer, while *S.p.* 'Royal Blue' is good with autumnal scarlets and reds. Giant-flowered *S.p.* 'Guanajuato' is in the original royal blue. Another must is *S. uliginosa*, with its sky-blue spikes. Grow, too, the early flowering *S. × superba*, with its treacly-purple flowers, and *S. guaranitica* in the darkest purple-blue. I also cut bright red *S. elegans* and *S. fulgens* to mix with oranges and ochres.

Of the many good annual salvias, look out for *S. viridis* with green-veined bracts of purple, blue or pink and *S. farinacea* 'Victoria', with its deep violet flowers; both are 45cm/18in tall.

CONDITIONING

Strip the bottom leaves of *S. patens*. For the others, sear the bottom 2.5cm/1in of stem and give a cool drink.

CULTIVATION

Plant sages in a sunny, well-protected site to get the maximum number of flowers. Most like plenty of moisture during summer, and the tender varieties especially need well-drained soil. Stake the tallest forms. Protect the underground roots of *S. uliginosa* in winter with straw.

Propagate more tender varieties from cuttings taken in late summer and overwintered in a frost-free cold frame or cool greenhouse. Dig up the parent plant, allow it to die down during the winter, and it will reshoot in spring. Plant out after the risk of frost has passed. For robust plants, treat *S. patens* as a half-hardy annual and sow every year. *S. uliginosa* and *S. × superba* are best propagated by division. Direct sow seed of the annuals in mid-spring.

(Left to right) *Salvia farinacea* 'Victoria', *S. patens, S. uliginosa*

OCTOBER

OCTOBER

ASTER
Daisy, Michaelmas daisy

Herbaceous perennial

ZONES: 5–10
HEIGHT: *A. amellus* 30cm/12in; *A. × frikartii* 'Mönch',
90cm/36in; *A. novi-belgii* 90–120cm/3–4ft

These frothy, single and double daisies come
in a full range of blue, purple, mauve and
white. I especially like the long-flowering, pale
mauve *A. × frikartii* 'Mönch' with its yellow
centre, the richer purple with yellow *A. amellus*
'Veilchenkönigin', the mid-purple *A. novi-belgii*
'Sailor Boy' and the deep cerise-pink *A.n.-b.*
'Carnival'. Arrange them mixed in a brilliant
colour jamboree with salvias and dahlias.

Strip the bottom leaves, give them a drink
overnight, and the flowers will last up to two weeks
in water. Grow asters in sun or partial shade, in
rich but well-drained soil. These plants are easy to
grow from softwood cuttings or division in spring.

Aster novi-belgii 'Carnival'

(Left to right)
Penstemon
'Hidcote Pink',
P. 'Blackbird'

PENSTEMON

**Evergreen herbaceous perennial
and subshrub**

ZONES: 8–10
HEIGHT AND SPREAD: 45–90cm/18–36in x 30–60cm/12–24in

The lovely flower spikes of the large-flowered border
penstemon hybrids, with their many tubular flowers arranged
up the stem like an array of trumpets, are a real mainstay of
the autumn cutting garden. Their velvety colours range from
white to pink, and bright scarlet to nearly black. My favourites
are *P.* 'Raven' or *P.* 'Blackbird' mixed with orange and yellow
red hot pokers (*Kniphofia*) and Chinese lanterns; the bluish-
purple *P.* 'Sour Grapes' and *P.* 'Stapleford Gem'; the clear
blue-mauve *P.* 'Blue Bedder'; and the lovely rich *P.* 'Burgundy'.

Some penstemons droop after cutting. Strip the bottom
leaves and sear the stem before soaking overnight.

Plant penstemons in full sun in fertile, well-drained soil,
facing south or west and well sheltered from wind. If you pick
or deadhead regularly, you will have 3–4 months of flowering
well into the autumn.

159

PROJECT FOR OCTOBER:

AN AUTUMN GIFT

This rich, bright, multicoloured bunch of flowers and leaves wrapped in clear cellophane will impress and cheer any friend or relation. With the carmine-pink, claret-red, clear turquoise and deep orange, all set against the silver and green of cyperus, artemisia and elaeagnus, it would be hard to beat this mixture for rich colour.

The cellophane looks good and protects the flowers for a journey.

EQUIPMENT
- twine
- clear cellophane
- florist's scissors

PLANTS
5–7 stems, 45cm/18in long, of each of the following:
- elaeagnus (*E. angustifolia* or *E.* 'Quicksilver')
- artemisia (*A. arborescens* 'Faith Raven' or *A. pontica*)
- bupleurum (*B. fruticosum*)
- iris seed heads (*I. foetidissima*)
- salvia (*S. uliginosa*)
- pennisetum (*P. villosum*)

5–7 stems, 30cm/12in long, of each of the following:
- dahlia (any two of *D.* 'Glow', 'Natal', 'Queen Fabiola' or 'Arabian Night')
- Michaelmas daisy (*Aster novi-belgii* 'Carnival')
- cyperus (*C. albostriatus* or *C. eragrostis*)

METHOD
Strip all the bottom leaves of the stems that you would expect to be below the waterline in the vase. Follow steps 1–4.

1 Make a structure in your hand from the elaeagnus and add the artemisia and bupleurum, leaving some elaeagnus stems standing proud. The foliage should be balanced yet not too symmetrical, with some stems curving down at the front.

2 Still holding the bunch in your hand, add the dahlias and Michaelmas daisies, distributing them evenly, and then poke in the iris seed heads.

3 Add the final touches of the contrasting sky-blue salvias, the bright green cyperus and feathery pennisetum, putting some at the heart and some at the edges of the bunch, so the arrangement is balanced and yet not neat. It will now be difficult to hold together so many stems.

4 Either get someone to help you by tying the stems as you hold them, or lay the bunch carefully on a table, hold it with one hand and tie it with the other and your teeth. Trim the stems to the same length. If you cut any woody stems, slit them again to about 2.5cm/1in so that they can still readily absorb water.

AUTUMN PLANTING

For many plants the demands of flowering are over in autumn, but they have not yet reached a dormant stage. This means that newly planted herbaceous perennials, shrubs and trees can put on some root growth before winter cold sets in. Autumn planting is most suitable for truly hardy plants such as alchemilla, stachys and astrantia that, even when young, can survive hard frosts.

- Plant well before frost is forecast. Frost endangers the tiny, fragile rootlets that are so important for water uptake.

- Give each plant a good soaking before you plant it by immersing the pot in a wheelbarrow filled with water. When the air bubbles stop, all the compost is wet. Water the plant in very well once it is in the ground, too.

- Always dig generous holes so that there is plenty of room to spread out the roots of each plant. Never cram the root ball into a confined space, or you will at best delay growth and at worst kill the plant. Mix some organic fertilizer into the bottom of the hole and spread some over the soil you replace around the new plant.

- For a large plant, firm the soil around the plant with your boot, so there are no large air pockets left. For a smaller plant, it is best to use your hands.

Astrantia major

OCTOBER

NOVEMBER

PLANNING THE CUTTING PATCH

This small area, 3m/10ft × 4.5m/15ft, stands in a sunny part of the garden. It is stocked with annuals and one or two biennials such as Iceland poppy. The colours and textures of the plants will guarantee a balanced arrangement from almost any combination.

THE DESIGN

The plan is straightforward: a series of rectangles with a central diamond-shaped bed and a sweet-pea wigwam as the focal point. Woven hurdles, 45cm/18in high, surround the beds and contain and support the plants. Alternatively, the beds could be edged with low, wooden picket fences. All parts of the beds are easily reached either from the central paths or from outside.

THE PLANTS

As long as they are cut or picked regularly, the plants will provide a continuous supply of foliage and flowers from late spring until the first frosts. They are easily grown from seed, but for those who prefer to buy in plants, most of them are available as seedlings from nurseries and garden centres. All are planted 20–25cm/8–10in apart. Cornflowers and scabious do not transplant well and are sown directly into the ground, and the seedlings thinned.

PREPARATION AND MAINTENANCE

Prepare the area in autumn. Seedlings should be planted out as soon as it is safe to do so in spring after the very last frost. Dense planting in blocks gives a lovely mosaic appearance and helps keep the weeds under control. When the plants are still small, fill gaps with a mulch of mushroom compost or well-rotted manure to inhibit weed seedlings and retain moisture. Feed and water regularly. Keep cutting, to stop the plants running to seed.

A rich, intense arrangement can be made from Nicotiana 'Lime Green', the deep blue larkspur Consolida Exquisite Series 'Blue Spire' and sumptuous Cosmos bipinnatus 'Dazzler'. This cosmos – one of my favourite plants for cutting – is perfect for the cutting patch as it earns its keep many times over, flowering from late spring until the end of autumn. Mix it too with green dill, both in the cutting patch and in the vase.

Plan of the plot

1. annual scabious (*Scabiosa atropurpurea*)
2. bishop's flower (*Ammi majus*)
3. cosmos (*C. bipinnatus* 'Purity') and snapdragons (*Antirrhinum majus* 'White Wonder')
4. bupleurum (*B. griffithii*) and bells of Ireland (*Moluccella laevis*)
5. snapdragons (*Antirrhinum majus* 'Black Prince') and arctotis (*A. fastuosa*)
6. black cornflowers (*Centaurea cyanus* 'Black Ball') and pot marigolds (*Calendula officinalis* Art Shades Group)
7. euphorbias (*E. palustris*) and Iceland poppies (*Papaver nudicaule*)
8. blue cornflowers (*Centaurea cyanus* 'Blue Diadem')
9. sweet peas (*Lathyrus odoratus*)
10. poppies (*Papaver rhoeas* 'Shirley Group') and love-in-a-mist (*Nigella*)
11. larkspur (*Consolida* Exquisite Series)
12. cosmos (*C. bipinnatus* 'Dazzler') and dill (*Anethum graveolens*)
13. sweet William (*Dianthus barbatus*) and tobacco plants (*Nicotiana* 'Lime Green')

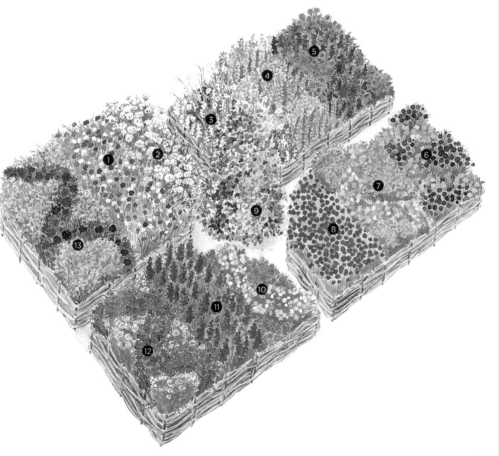

EXTENDING THE PICKING SEASON

After clearing the cutting patch in autumn, plant it with
bulbs for harvesting from early spring through to the
beginning of summer, when the annuals take over. Choose
hyacinths, scillas, tulips and narcissi and, after picking,
lift the bulbs. Also, make effective use of the ground by
doubling up the planting of the patch. For example,
replace the early flowerers such as sweet Williams, which
tend to be over by midsummer, with a selection of pot-
reared dahlias and penstemons. These will give you rich-
coloured flowers right through to the first frosts.

*When you plant an
annual cutting patch,
think of arranging the
colours as you might in a
bunch of flowers. Here,
sweet peas, cornflowers
and poppies make good
partners to pincushion
flower* (Scabiosa
atropurpurea), *while
the black cornflower*
Centaurea cyanus
'Black Ball' *provides a
brilliant contrast to pot
marigolds* (Calendula
officinalis *Art
Shades Group*).

*Nearby, rich crimson
snapdragons*
(Antirrhinum majus
'Black Prince') *are
interplanted with burnt-
orange* Arctotis fastuosa
(which is nearly over).
Antirrhinum majus
'White Wonder' *mixes with
anything, in the garden or
in an arrangement, while
bupleurum,* Euphorbia
palustris, *bells of Ireland*
(Moluccella laevis)
and globe artichokes
(Cynara cardunculus
Scolymus Group) *provide
interesting foliage.*

NOVEMBER

NERINE

Bulb

ZONES: 8–10
HEIGHT: 45–60cm/18–24in

VARIETIES GOOD
FOR CUTTING

I used to have an aversion to nerine. The hardiest, the harsh nail-varnish pink *N. bowdenii*, often shouts too loudly from its sunny flower bed. You can have fun with them, though. Place in a vase for a fabulous modern still life, or mix it with bright green cyperus, shrubby bupleurum and sky-blue *Salvia uliginosa*. Avoid a conventional mix with whites and blues. There are some beautiful but tender cultivars. Try deeper pink, large-flowered *N. bowdenii* 'Mark Fenwick' or the white *N. undulata* Flexuosa Group 'Alba'. Mix the even more brazen salmon-orangey-pink colour forms with crimson-black dahlias and Chinese lanterns.

CONDITIONING

Give nerine a good drink and they will last for more than a week in water.

CULTIVATION

Plant the hardy varieties in late summer or after flowering, with the noses of the bulbs showing above the soil. Choose a sheltered site, in full sun, preferably with the shelter and warmth of a sunny wall. They do best on light, sandy soil. Grow the more tender forms in a greenhouse, and plant out after the risk of frosts has disappeared.

The leaves appear after the flower spike and disappear by the summer. To get the best flowers, water until the leaves die down, then let them dry off. Protect with a good mulch through winter. Nerine dislike being disturbed, but as they become congested lift and replant every 4–5 years in autumn or when the leaves die down. They can also be grown from fresh seed.

Nerine bowdenii 'Mark Fenwick'

AMELANCHIER
Canadian shadbush, Juneberry,
Serviceberry, Snowy mespilus

Deciduous shrub and tree

ZONES: 5-9
HEIGHT AND SPREAD: 6m/20ft x 3m/10ft

Amelanchier
lamarckii

There is widespread confusion between the commonly
available amelanchiers – *A. canadensis*, *A. laevis* and
A. lamarckii – which are in fact so very similar that even
botanists argue about which is which. So never mind its
label in the nursery, just look out for the shrub or small
tree that has fine, oval leaves and an overall delicate
structure and form. I love the combination in mid-spring
of newly emerging, copper-coloured foliage with white
blossom – a chalky-white cloud of fine flowers, until the
wind blows them away. I use it as the main structure in
a huge spring mixture of white lilac, Viridiflora tulips,
white pompon peonies and the white bleeding heart
Lamprocapnos spectabilis 'Alba'. Amelanchier proves its
worth again in autumn, with its small leaves turning an
iridescent mix of reds, oranges and ochres.

PHYSALIS ALKEKENGI
Chinese lantern

Physalis alkekengi

Herbaceous perennial

ZONES: 5-8
HEIGHT: 60cm/24in

Physalis is invaluable for filling in awkward
corners, since it will thrive in sun or shade and is
not fussy about soil. But when you choose the
site do bear in mind that the running roots
of physalis can become invasive, so they
should be kept well away from your more
delicate plants. The tall stems tend to flop
but can be held up by a network of sticks
and thin twine or thread.

Propagate by division in autumn or
spring, planting the tendrily roots 8cm/3in
deep, or sow seed in early spring. It will fruit in
the autumn of the same year.

171

PROJECT FOR NOVEMBER:

RED HOT LEAVES

This late harvest of sprays of leaves, berries, hips changing colour, and bulrushes includes just a few dahlia, delphinium, salvia and leonotis flowers. Let the foliage go in all directions, with no careful harmony of colour or texture – a mound of dazzling red leaves and remaining splashes of flower colour contrasting with the white snowberries.

EQUIPMENT
- pewter jug, 30cm/12in tall
- glass fisherman's floats
- large Christmas baubles

PLANTS
5 each of the following stems, 60–90cm/24–36in long:
- smokebush (*Cotinus obovatus*)
- oak (*Quercus rubra*)
- bulrushes (*Typha*)

7–11 stems, 45–75cm/18–30in long, of each of the following:
- euphorbia (*E. griffithii* 'Fireglow' or 'Dixter')
- rose hips (*Rosa* 'Geranium' or *Rosa rugosa*)
- snowberry berries (*Symphoricarpos albus*)

5–7 stems, 60–90cm/24–36in long, of each of the following flowers:
- delphinium (*D.* Black Knight Group)
- leonotis (*L. ocymifolia*)
- dahlias (*D.* 'Edinburgh')
- blue salvias (*S. guaranitica* or *S. farinacea* 'Victoria')
- red salvias (*S. elegans* or *S. fulgens*)

METHOD
Using the smokebush and oak stems, make a framework about twice the height of the jug. Add the euphorbias to fill in any gaping holes. Place the vertical emphasis next, using the bulrushes, delphiniums and leonotis, so that the arrangement does not become too round and ordered. Then arrange the hips and berries fairly symmetrically, so no area is left out. Use the heavy hips to curve over the lip of the jug. Finally, add the dahlias and salvias at the centre.

FORCING BULBS

- Pot the bulbs up in plastic pots that will fit into a terracotta or ceramic flower pot. When one potful dies you can just remove it and replace it with a fresh one.

- Once potted, store bulbs in moist compost, in a cold, dark place. This will encourage strong root growth before the leaves and flowers develop. Narcissi, an exception, need cold, but not dark, for strong growth to start.

- Pot your bulbs up in several different batches, so that the flowering season is extended.

LAYERING SHRUBS

- Propagate plants such as witch hazel and philadelphus that have low-lying branches by layering. Simply bend down a healthy, vigorous lower branch so that it can touch the ground. Dig out a 5cm/2in trench about 25cm/10in from the tip of the branch. Strip the leaves and side shoots except at the tip and pin the branch into the trench with a hairpin-shaped piece of wire. Cover it with soil and wait for roots to form. The following spring, sever the branch from the parent and you will have an independent offspring. After a month, dig it up and replant it.

DIGGING UP AND DIVIDING HERBACEOUS PERENNIALS

- You can divide herbaceous perennials as successfully in autumn as in spring. The hardier perennials can be planted out straight away. With the more delicate plants, it is best to play safe and nurture the new offspring for a while, potting them up and putting them in a cold frame for protection until spring.

- Dig up your tender perennials, such as salvias and penstemons, and overwinter them in a frost-free cold frame or greenhouse.

- Move biennials that were sown during the summer to their final flowering positions in early autumn. Dig them up individually, trying to dislodge as little soil as possible from their roots to preserve the smallest fragile rootlets. Water them in and keep moist.

- The ground may be drier in autumn so, to make the root ball and soil stick together in one big clod, give the clump a good soaking before digging it up. With more soil sticking to the roots, you damage the tiny delicate rootlets less and so give the transplanted offspring a better start.

NOVEMBER

DECEMBER

VIBURNUM

Deciduous and evergreen shrub

ZONES: *V. x bodnantense, V. sargentii* 7–8;
V. x burkwoodii, V. carlesii, V. opulus 5–8;
V. farreri 6–8; *V. tinus* 8–10
HEIGHT AND SPREAD: *V. carlesii, V. farreri,
V. opulus* 'Compactum' 1.5m/5ft x 1.5m/5ft;
V. x burkwoodii varieties 2.5m/8ft x 2.5m/8ft;
V. x bodnantense varieties 3m/10ft x 2m/7ft;
V. sargentii, V. tinus 3m/10ft x 3m/10ft

VARIETIES GOOD FOR CUTTING

As a family, the viburnums have to be in
my top ten for year-round picking – the
winter-flowerers are certainly mainstays of
the winter cutting garden. The evergreen
laurustinus (*V. tinus*), with its white or pink
flower heads, is good in arrangements of
any size. For smaller bunches, though, I tend
to strip some of the leaves, otherwise the
overall effect may be too dense. Metallic-
blue berries, left over from the previous year
of flowering, are a bonus of this handsome
shrub, while pale pink *V.t.* 'Gwenllian' has
the best berries of all.

Highly recommended for larger gardens
are varieties of the winter-flowering *V. ×
bodnantense*, such as *V. × b.* 'Dawn', with deep
pink buds and paler pink flowers, and *V. ×
b.* 'Deben', with white flowers tinted pink.
Both last well when cut, and their clumps of
white or pale pink flowers on bare branches
are ideal at the bedside – wake to enjoy their
gentle scent. *V. farreri* (syn. *V. fragrans*) does
not last so well and its flowers tend to drop.
Varieties of the late winter and spring-
flowering *V. × burkwoodii* and of *V. carlesii* are
also pretty and scented. Good in late spring
and early summer is *V. opulus* 'Roseum', and
in autumn the wild form of *V. opulus* with its
red, orange or yellow berries.

(Left to right) *Viburnum × bodnantense* 'Dawn', *V. × burkwoodii*

CONDITIONING

Give them a good drink and they will last for
more than a week in water.

CULTIVATION

All viburnums thrive in any fertile, moist soil
and most grow happily on lime or acid soils.
Plant them in late autumn in sun or semi-
shade and mulch in late winter. In general,
viburnums do not need pruning, but when
you cut branches for the house do so with the
resulting shape of the bush in mind. With big
shrubs like these, I recommend buying one
specimen, as it takes years before you can
pick from newly propagated plants. If you
are patient, you can take semi-ripe cuttings
in summer and insert them in a sandy mix.

CORNUS
Dogwood, Cornel

Mainly deciduous shrub and tree

ZONES: 2–8 except *C. mas* 5–8
HEIGHT AND SPREAD: *C. alba* 'Elegantissima',
C.a. 'Sibirica' to 2m/7ft x 2m/7ft; *C. sericea*
'Flaviramea' to 2m/7ft x 4m/13ft; *C. mas* to
5.5m/18ft x 5.5m/18ft

Most dogwoods are tough plants and thrive
almost anywhere, but *C. mas* prefers a sunny,
sheltered position against a wall. Plant in
early winter.

If left to their own devices all dogwoods
become large shrubs or small trees. Like
willows, their size can be kept in check by
coppicing in late winter and by regular
cutting. If you are growing them for their
winter stems cut them back in early spring
every year or every two years, since it is the
new growth that provides the bright colour.

You can take softwood cuttings in summer
or hardwood cuttings in autumn or winter.

HAMAMELIS
Witch hazel

Deciduous shrub

ZONES: 5–9
HEIGHT AND SPREAD: 2.5–3m/8–10ft x
2.5m/8ft

All the witch hazels, with their spidery,
frost-proof flowers, like the tentacles of a sea
anemone, are lovely cut and last up to two
weeks in water. Place three branches in a
vase and put it where you can enjoy the faint
but delicious scent. *H.* × *intermedia* 'Pallida'
is the best yellow-flowered form, but *H.* × *i.*
'Jelena' has more delicate flowers.

Plant in moist but well-drained, neutral
to acid soil (they will grow on lime but not
chalk). Most like a sunny, open site, though
H. × *intermedia* thrives in semi-shade. They
are slow growers, but you can propagate by
layering in autumn.

Cornus mas

Hamamelis ×
intermedia 'Pallida'

179

PROJECT FOR DECEMBER:

A WINTER MEDALLION

This dramatic yet simple wall hanging is easy to make. You can leave it hanging for many months, decorating it with fresh flowers whenever you have some. I have chosen hellebores, but *Narcissus* 'Paper White' or *Iris unguicularis* will look equally lovely.

Before you construct the medallion, decide where you are going to hang it and put a hook in the wall. Work out how large you want the finished medallion to be, according to the expanse of wall.

EQUIPMENT

- strong 3mm/1/8in binding wire
- fine-gauge florist's wire
- florist's scissors
- wire cutters
- odourless hair spray, for holding clematis seed heads in place
- 10–15 small florist's water vials (optional)
- a tack or picture hook for hanging the medallion

PLANTS

10–15 stems, 90cm/36in long, of each of the following:

- pliable willow, e.g. weeping willow (*Salix babylonica*); red or yellow dogwood (*Cornus*) makes a good alternative
- violet willow (*Salix daphnoides*) or pussy willow (*S. caprea*)

10–15 stems, about 45–60cm/18–24in long, of each of the following:

- hazel (*Corylus*) or other catkins; alder (*Alnus*) makes a good alternative
- old man's beard (*Clematis vitalba*) seed heads; any fluffy clematis seed heads, such as *C. tangutica* or *C.* 'Bill MacKenzie', are fine
- 10–15 stems of hellebores (*Helleborus* x *hybridus*), 30cm/12in long

1 Form a wire circle from the binding wire and fasten the ends with fine-gauge wire. Bend three pliable willow or dogwood stems around the wire hoop, weaving them in and out. These willow stems will hold themselves in place once you have wired their thicker ends on to the circle; you can then tuck in their whippier ends.

2 Starting at a different spot, add more stems, poking the cut ends into the willow framework. Always weave the willow around the wire in the same direction to create a regular shape. Add further branches until you have constructed a substantial base. Bind the branches together firmly with the fine-gauge wire.

3 Add all the violet or pussy willow stems, one at a time, winding them around the base and poking in the ends. Again, make sure you weave them in the same direction as the first willow or dogwood stems. With the fine-gauge wire, secure the main stems of violet or pussy willow.

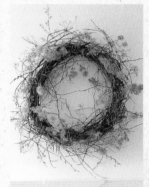

4 Add the catkins, poking them in randomly and at different angles; so that the medallion doesn't look too stiff and formal.

5 Hang the medallion on the wall. If the circle looks at all asymmetrical or out of shape, carefully bend it back into a circle.

6 Insert branches of old man's beard at random intervals, taking care not to knock off its fragile seed heads. If you want the flowers to last longer than a few hours, insert their stems into the florist's water vials before adding them to the medallion. The vials can be hidden among the willow branches.

PREPARING THE GARDEN FOR WINTER

- Tidy dead foliage, prune and mulch; also wrap or even dig up to bring inside frost-tender plants.

- As some plants brown and die, cut them back to the ground so they can emerge green and fresh without having to push through their decaying leaves the following spring.

- Leave some plants whose dead foliage and flower or seed heads are an asset to the winter garden. Teasels, acanthus and alliums look good through the winter.

- Spread a layer of manure or home-made compost over the whole garden and dig it in. If your soil is heavy, leave any large clods – they will be better broken up by the winter weather than by your struggling with them now. Lighten your soil by spreading some horticultural grit or sharp sand. Never walk over newly dug ground or you will undo all the good soil structuring you have done. Lay a plank down and stand on this if you need to go over the ground again.

Thistles in frost

DECEMBER

GROWING SHRUBS, TREES AND YEAR-ROUND FOLIAGE

Many of the foliage plants here are used as structural stems in starting arrangements. But there are also a few beauty queens, such as callicarpa and euonymus, to use on their own. Evergreens provide material all year round, but avoid the deadening greens such as laurel (*Prunus laurocerasus* and *P. lusitanica*) – used by many florists.

MAPLE (*Acer platanoides*)

A. platanoides and *A.p.* 'Crimson King' are bright and fresh with their acid-green and yellow flowers and red or bright green newly emerging leaves. Mix with spring bulbs or anemones. The red and yellow colours of *A.p.* 'Crimson King' are the perfect complement to bright Parrot tulips.

HORSE CHESTNUT (*Aesculus hippocastanum*)

The sticky buds of the horse chestnut tree emerge from tight bud into luscious green, new leaves. Cut boughs, and watch the buds emerging on their own, or mix them with strong and flamboyant flowers such as the Parrot tulips, which parade their huge, frilly flowers at the same time in spring.

ALDER (*Alnus*)

During late winter the elongating, rich brown-purple catkins and small cones of *A. cordata* make a lovely structure for any big vase. Mix with sumptuous amaryllis or simply with a great haze of pussy willow.

CALLICARPA

The tiny, pinhead, purple berries of *C. bodinieri* have a brightness and beauty that make them look like a peculiar, poisonous sort of medicine. They are at their best in late autumn when the leaves have been shed, with only the brilliant violet berries remaining on their slim branches. The berries look good on their own in a bright and contrasting orange or turquoise vase but they also mix spectacularly with orange dahlias. They will last for more than a month before wrinkling.

HORNBEAM (*Carpinus*)

Whether you pick hornbeam with its early spring catkins or wait until the summer when its seed cases hang from the tree like upside-down pagodas, this tree with its exciting and unusual foliage will enhance any arrangement. Alternatively, you could cut off the leaves and use the bright lime-green seed cases as the 'foliage' to mix with poppies, cornflowers and lavender in a multicoloured summer swag. Or exploit the elegance of hornbeam by cutting great tall branches to enhance any large vase.

MEXICAN ORANGE BLOSSOM (*Choisya*)

Whether you choose the ordinary, luscious, shiny bottle-green variety, *C. ternata*, or the bright yellow-green-leaved *C.t.* 'Sundance', Mexican orange blossom has excellent long-lasting foliage. Pick it in spring for its scented flowers, too.

DOGWOOD (*Cornus alba*)

Cornus is an invaluable shrub for the cutting garden. *C. alba* colours up beautifully in autumn, and you can use its bright, bare branches in winter too. The fresh, white-bordered leaves of *C.a.* 'Elegantissima' are excellent in summer for mixing in a white and green arrangement. Use its strong upright habit as your main foliage structure.

TEASEL (*Dipsacus*)

The great spiny spikes of common teasel (*D. fullonum*, syn. *D. sylvestris*) when used as a green bud or displaying the whorls of pale mauve flowers are impressive sculptural features on their own or when mixed with luscious bunches of lilies.

OLEASTER (*Elaeagnus*)

Silver-leaved, olive-like, deciduous *E. angustifolia* and *E. commutata* are beautiful and elegant when used in summer or autumn arrangements. They go perfectly with my favourite crimsons, lapis lazuli or sky-blues and oranges.

GUM (*Eucalyptus*)

A multitude of eucalyptus varieties is available, providing invaluable foliage through the winter. Use sprigs of eucalyptus to lighten an arrangement of green and white. Cut larger stems to arrange on their own.

SPINDLE (*Euonymus*)

The common spindle tree *E. europaeus* has attractive fruits in autumn, and as the fruits ripen the hanging purses open and reveal the wonderful, contrasting, orange seeds contained in their vibrant pink, fleshy carapace. Arrange them on their own with many large boughs in a jug for the centre of a table, or use them simply as foliage with other pinks and greens.

IVY (*Hedera*)

Delicate bird's foot ivy (*H. helix* 'Pedata') is my favourite among the ivy family. Trail it across the table for a winter dinner or arrange it twisting and turning out from a tied bunch. In the autumn the black, shiny berries of the wild form of *H. helix* make a useful addition to an arrangement.

PRIVET (*Ligustrum*)

Many privet species have dull foliage but it may be worth planting the golden variety *L. ovalifolium* 'Aureum' or silver *L.o.* 'Argenteum' to use as background foliage in large arrangements.

APPLE, CRABAPPLE (*Malus*)

The white-flushed, pink blossom of the apple *M. domestica* 'Ribston Pippin' is to me a symbol of spring. Cut a few of its gnarled and knotted branches to have on their own. Crabapple *M.* 'John Downie' is another beauty, providing pure white blossom. In late summer and autumn this fruit tree family comes into its own again with many of the crabapples such as *M.* 'Golden Hornet'; even the smaller apples are fine companions to early autumn flowers.

Euonymus europaeus

PITTOSPORUM

P. tenuifolium, with its small, wrinkly-edged, greyish-green leaves, and *P.* 'Garnettii', a variegated hybrid with white-flushed, pink margins around the leaves, are a great source of foliage throughout the winter. Deep crimson *P. tenuifolium* 'Purpureum' is a perfect background plant to zingy oranges and acid-greens at any time of year.

CHERRY, PLUM, BLACKTHORN, SLOE (*Prunus*)

P. 'Taihaku', my favourite tree for spring cutting, is a must if you have room for it. Its huge, white, saucer-shaped flowers drop a dense cloud of white confetti like a snow storm in spring. The species *P. avium* with its smaller, dense collections of flowers is a lovely companion for any spring flower you care to name. Blackthorn (*P. spinosa*) also bears a pretty Japanese-style blossom that is light on the eye. This doubly earns its keep, for in autumn the black-smeared, blue sloes are set against the panther-blue-black of the spiny stems. Combine this with the rich chocolate, oranges and yellows of rudbeckias, sunflowers and autumn dahlias.

OAK (*Quercus*)

Red oak (*Q. rubra*), with its mixture of green, chestnut-brown, orange and red leaves, is enough arranged on its own in a vase in the autumn, or use it as your foliage for any great dahlia, salvia and gladioli arrangement. The copper, brown and ochre leaves of oak trees are excellent as a base for many huge autumn vases. The bright green acorns of English oak (*Q. robur*) are invaluable when mixed with crabapples and sunflowers for a glamorous yet relaxed vase.

RHAMNUS

The white-margined evergreen *R. alaternus* 'Argenteovariegata' is unusual in its tolerance of shade and is an invaluable filler for your winter and early spring bunches.

RUE (*Ruta graveolens*)

Rue is almost alone in its delicacy among the evergreen plants that can provide foliage at the leaner times of year. It can cause skin allergies, so wear rubber gloves when cutting and arranging it, particularly on a hot, sunny day.

WHITEBEAM (*Sorbus aria*)

The chiselled, deeply veined, silver-grey leaves of *S.a.* 'Lutescens' are perfect to lighten up any mixed spring vase. Pick them in bud to open out gradually, revealing their fresh grey upper surface and silver underside.

SNOWBERRY (*Symphoricarpos albus*)

Snowberry, which is a scraggy shrub usually associated with hedges and wild gardens, has milky white, often pink-flushed berries like helium balloons hanging on the ends of narrow, pliable twigs. Pick them through autumn and on into the winter to freshen up your heavy, hot colours.

Symphoricarpos albus

DECEMBER

PHOTOGRAPHIC ACKNOWLEDGMENTS

Photographs by Pia Tryde, with exception of the following;

Shutterstock:
Project pages background © MaxyM
Wallpaper background patterns; pages 9–21 © Magnia,
  23–35 © Yaviki; 37–51 © Pim; 53–67 © Cristatus; 69–85
  © Chantall; 87–103 © Nikifiva; 105–121 © rvika; 123–151
  © Markovka; 153–163 © Alla.ya; 165–175 © Parisian;
  177–187 © Ivan Negin
Salix p14 © Ruslan Kudvin; Camellia p20 © Anastasios71;
  Cyclamen p30 © Scisetti Alfio;

Snowdrop p31 © Stocksolutions; Rose p34 © Pete
Pahham, Japonica p47 © Stephane Bidouze; Hyacinth
p47 © Tom Viggars; Dicentra p80 © dabjola;
Lilac p80 © Stocksnapper; Dill p113 © Africa Studio;
Snapdragon p117 © Tamara Kulikova;
Rudbeckia p120 © Pavels; Felicia p136 © Jane McIlroy;
Gladioli p142 © An Nguyen; Penstemon p159 ©
Tamara Kulikova; Astrantia p162 © B. Isberg;
Physalis p171 © Coprid; Cornus mas p179 © Jopelka;
Thistle p182 © Montypeter.